Collins · do brilliantly!

EightWeeksFlat

KS3Science

Ian Pritchard

INTRODUCTION

Does this sound like you?
You know you should have started earlier but you haven't. The National Tests are just a few weeks away and you haven't even thought about revising because you thought you had ages. Or is it because you hate the whole revision thing – hours of staring at dull text books and badly taken class notes? Well don't despair, help is at hand in the form of *Eight Weeks Flat KS3 Science*.

Why Eight Weeks Flat?
This colourful, easy-to-follow revision guide will help you prepare for those important Tests. The book covers material at levels 4, 5 and 6 and is mainly designed for students hoping to gain a level 5 or 6 in Science at Key Stage 3.

Eight Weeks Flat KS3 Science follows a week-by-week, day-by-day plan to help you break down your revision into small chunks. The plan is designed to spread your revision out into 40 sessions to be completed over eight weeks. However, if you started a bit earlier, follow the plan but you can give yourself an occasional day off or use the time to redo a topic you are not so sure about. If you have cut it a bit fine by leaving yourself less than eight weeks, aim to cover two topics each evening or do some at the weekends too.

How Eight Weeks Flat works
Each weekday you tackle a different topic. Each revision session consists of a page of important subject content and a page of follow-up practice activities.

Start by reading the notes, important facts, tips and examples on the topic. Try to learn any facts you need to remember. This should take you a few minutes. Words in **bold** appear in the Glossary on pages 91–92. If you are not sure of the meaning of any of them, look them up!

When you think you are ready, turn over the page and try to answer all the questions. The questions include some easy ones as well as some more difficult ones. Try them all – you don't get any marks for questions you miss out. You may wish to set yourself a time to complete the questions. This may help you to focus on attempting the questions rather than staring at the wall. Why not promise yourself a treat when you've finished?

Detailed answers are provided at the back of the book (see page 93). Mark your answers or get someone at home to do it for you. Add up your score and see how you have done. Use the 'How did you score?' box at the bottom of each question page to help judge your performance.

After you have completed all 40 revision sessions, have a go at the practice test (see page 85). This test includes questions on most topics. It starts with the easier questions and gets more difficult towards the end. Allow yourself 40 minutes to complete it.

Ask someone to mark your practice test or do it yourself. Add up your marks and use the Level table at the end of the mark scheme (see page 96) to help decide the level you achieved. Remember – this is just an indication of your actual level.

If you have worked your way through the book and still have some time left for revision, go back and have another go at some of the sessions you didn't do so well the first time.

Best of luck!

About the National Tests
Just in case you are not sure how it all works, here is some information about the actual Tests.

At the beginning of May in Year 9 you will sit National Tests in Science (as well as in English and Maths). The Tests are available in two tiers – levels 3–6 and levels 5–7. Your teacher will decide which tier to enter you for. You will take two Tests altogether:

Paper 1	60 marks	1 hour
Paper 2	60 marks	1 hour

In each Test the questions get harder as you work through them. Make sure you have the correct equipment with you for each Test. You are expected to have a pen, pencil, ruler and eraser.

The completed Tests are sent away to be marked. You should find out how you have done early in July. Most Year 9 pupils get a level 5 or 6 in the Science National Tests.

CONTENTS

REVISION CHECKLIST

	Page numbers	Revised?
Scientific enquiry		
Scientific questions	pages 77-78	
Plan and design experiments	pages 79-80	
Obtain and present evidence	pages 81-82	
Consider and evaluate evidence	pages 83-84	
Life processes and living things		
Cells	pages 5-6	
Reproduction	pages 7-8	
Feeding relationships	pages 9-10	
Variation and classification	pages 11-12	
Food and digestion	pages 29-30	
Respiration	pages 31-32	
Microbes and disease	pages 33-34	
Ecological relationships	pages 35-36	
Inheritance and selection	pages 53-54	
Fit and healthy	pages 55-56	
Plants and photosynthesis	pages 57-58	
Plants for food	pages 59-60	
Materials and their properties		
Acids and alkalis	pages 13-14	
Simple chemical reactions	pages 15-16	
Particle model of matter	pages 17-18	
Solutions	pages 19-20	
Electrical circuits	pages 23-24	
Atoms and elements	pages 37-38	
Compounds and mixtures	pages 39-40	
Rocks and weathering	pages 41-42	
The rock cycle	pages 43-44	
Heating and cooling	pages 45-46	
Reactions with metals	pages 61-62	
Patterns of reactivity	pages 63-64	
Chemistry in the environment	pages 65-66	
Using chemistry	pages 67-68	
Physical processes		
Energy resources	pages 21-22	
Forces and their effects	pages 25-26	
The solar system and beyond	pages 27-28	
Magnets and electromagnets	pages 47-48	
Light	pages 49-50	
Sound and hearing	pages 51-52	
Energy and electricity	pages 69-70	
Gravity and space	pages 71-72	
Speed and streamlining	pages 73-74	
Pressure and moments	pages 75-76	

CELLS

Week 1
Monday

What you need to know

1. Know that **cells** are the basic units of life.
2. Know that some cells are organised into **tissues** from which **organs** are made.
3. Know about the structure of cells and the key differences between plant and animal cells.
4. Know some functions of cells.

CELL FACTS

- **Cells** are the basic 'building blocks' of all living things. They are very small and come in many different shapes and sizes depending on what job they do.
- In your body you have many types of cells including nerve cells, blood cells and skin cells.

TWO TYPES OF CELL

- Cells are grouped into two different types:
  - Cells that can make copies of themselves. They have a **nucleus** that contains all of the information they need.
  - Cells that need to link with another cell before they can make copies. These are called sex cells and they only contain half the information needed to make copies.

LINKING CELLS

- Bacteria have only one cell in their body. They are called unicellular.
- However, animals and plants are multicellular. They need to have many cells because they are complicated organisms.
- Groups of cells of the same type link together to make **tissues**. **Organs** contain different tissues.
- Cells have different shapes depending on which kind of tissue they are in, and what job they do.

ANIMAL AND PLANT CELLS

	Animal cell	**Plant cell**
Nucleus which controls what the cell does	yes	yes
Surface membrane	yes	yes
Vacuoles that contain liquid	very small	one large
Cytoplasm where chemical processes happen	yes	yes
Strong cell wall	no	yes

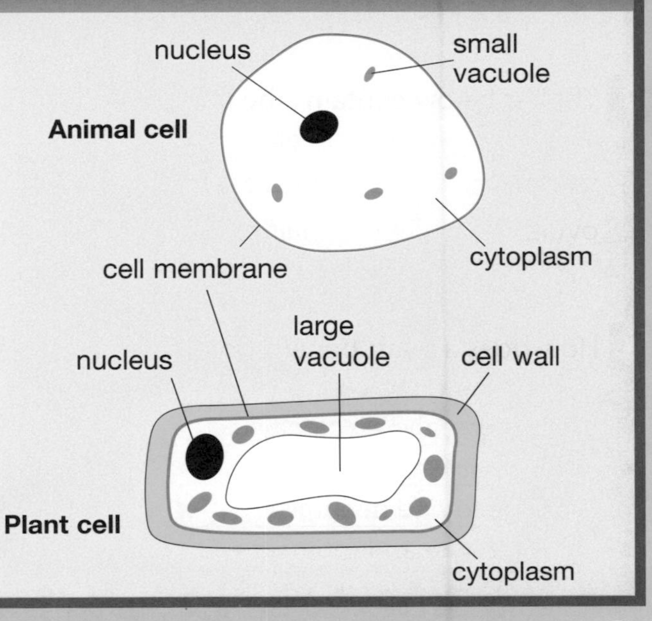

CELLS

1 Name **three** different cells from your body.

3 marks

2 What is special about 'sex cells'?

1 mark

3 What is special about the cells in a tissue?

1 mark

4 An organ contains more than one type of tissue. True or false?

1 mark

5 List **three** similarities between animal and plant cells.

3 marks

6 List **two** differences between animal and plant cells.

2 marks

7 Look at the diagrams of an animal and a plant cell. What labels would you use for the parts indicated?

8 marks

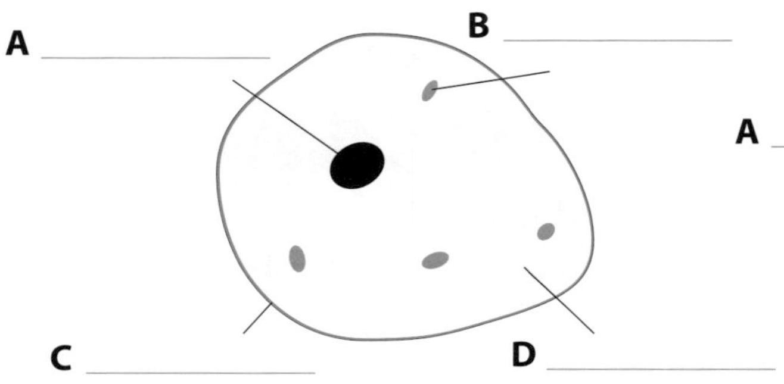

A
B
C
D

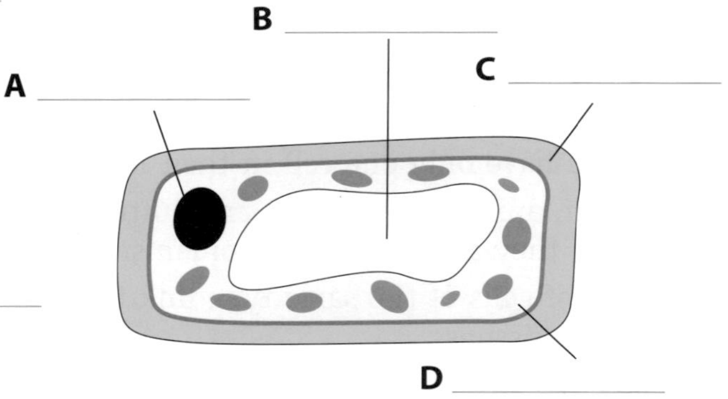

A
B
C
D

8 Humans and trees are 'multicellular' organisms. Explain what 'multicellular' means.

1 mark

9 The list below contains the names of eight types of cell. Underline the sex cells.

sperm	nerve	skin	leaf
ovule	hair root	pollen grain	ovum

4 marks

10 How does a plant benefit from having a strong cell wall?

1 mark

TOTAL

How did you score?

10 or less – try again!
11 – 19 – nearly there!
20 – 25 – well done!

REPRODUCTION

Week 1 Tuesday

What you need to know

1. Know the way the human body changes during puberty.
2. Know how changes in the human body are linked to human reproduction, growth and the **menstrual cycle**.
3. Know about human reproduction and how offspring are protected and nurtured.

CHANGES DURING PUBERTY

- Puberty is when your body begins to prepare itself for reproduction and adult life.

For females, this means:

- breasts enlarge;
- more body hair grows;
- the overall shape of the body changes;
- ovaries begin to release ova (unfertilised eggs) at a rate of approximately one a month. This is called **ovulation**;
- if the ovum is not **fertilised**, the uterus lining is not needed and is released in a process called menstruation;
- there are emotional and behavioural changes.

For males:

- the penis increases in size;
- testes start to produce sperm;
- more body hair grows;
- the voice deepens;
- the overall shape of the body changes;
- there are emotional and behavioural changes.

BECOMING PREGNANT

- If a male and female have sexual intercourse, sperm from the male enters the female and may reach an ovum.
- If the sperm enters the ovum and fertilises it, then the single cell that has been formed has all the information it needs to become a baby.
- The cell must then keep dividing to become an embryo, and attach itself to the wall of the uterus.

NURTURING A BABY

- Inside the mother the uterus develops a placenta which enables waste products to leave the growing embryo and nutrients to be passed to it.
- After two months, the embryo has grown to become a **fetus**.
- After nine months the fetus has become a baby and is ready to be born.
- Meanwhile hormones are released in the female that make the mammary glands in her breasts start to produce milk for the baby to drink when it is born.

Flow diagram showing the stages of pregnancy

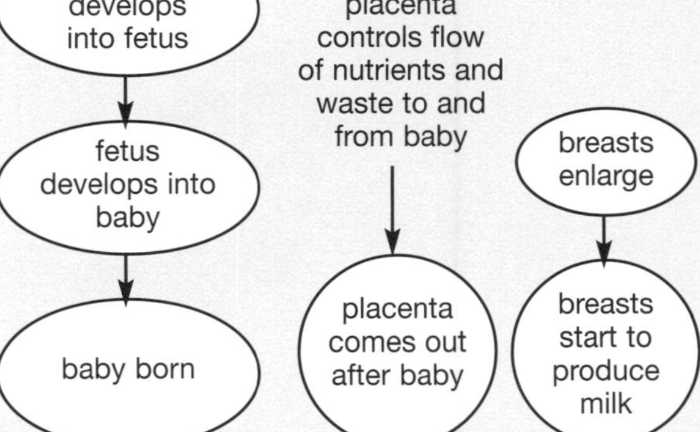

REPRODUCTION

1 List the changes that happen in the body of a female during puberty.

3 marks

2 List the changes that happen in the body of a male during puberty.

2 marks

3 A sperm's head contains enzymes that break down cell membranes. Explain why sperm need these enzymes.

1 mark

4 Give **two** reasons why a woman does not become pregnant every time she has sex with a man.

2 marks

5 The placenta has **two** functions. What are they?

2 marks

6 Join the words on the left to their correct description.

6 marks

ovulation	an unfertilised egg
menstruation	the process of releasing an immature egg
ovary	a number of unfertilised eggs
uterus	the place where immature eggs are stored
ovum	the place where a fertilised egg embeds itself to grow
ova	monthly bleeding when the uterus lining is shed

7 Here is a partly labelled diagram of the female reproductive organs. Complete the labels.

5 marks

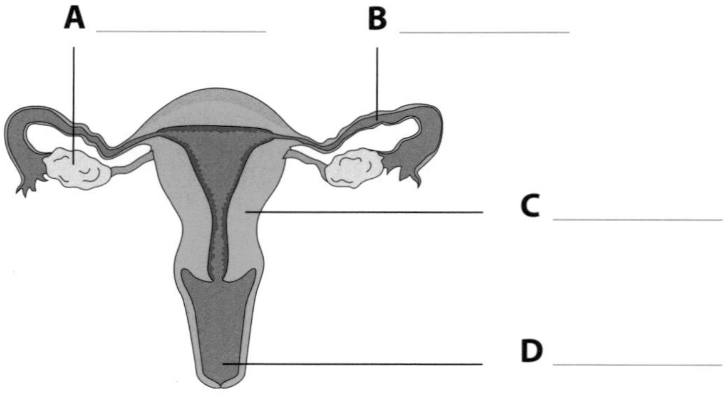

A ______ B ______

C ______

D ______

8 Here is a partly labelled diagram of the male reproductive organs. Complete the labels.

4 marks

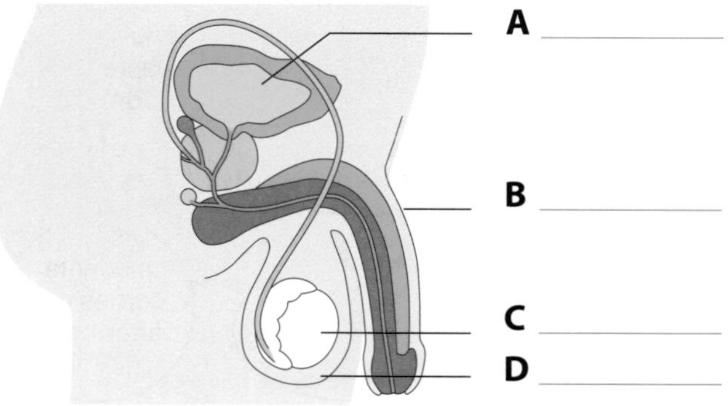

A ______

B ______

C ______

D ______

TOTAL

How did you score?

10 or less – try again!

11 – 19 – nearly there!

20 – 25 – well done!

FEEDING RELATIONSHIPS

Week 1 Wednesday

What you need to know

1. Know that there are a variety of **habitats**.
2. Know how plants and animals are adapted to live in a particular habitat.
3. Know about **adaptations** for feeding.
4. Know how plants and animals interact with each other, including feeding relationships.
5. Know how to link **food chains** to make food webs.

MANY KINDS OF HABITAT

- A **habitat** is a place where plants and animals live.
- There are many kinds of habitats, such as deserts, rainforests and oceans.

ANIMALS AND PLANTS MUST BE SUITED TO THEIR HABITAT

- Animals and plants have to be suited to the habitat in which they live or they will not survive.
- As well as being suited to the climate of the habitat, animals and plants must be adapted to other animals and plants in the habitat.
- Animals must have **adaptations** that allow them to eat other plants and animals in their habitat.

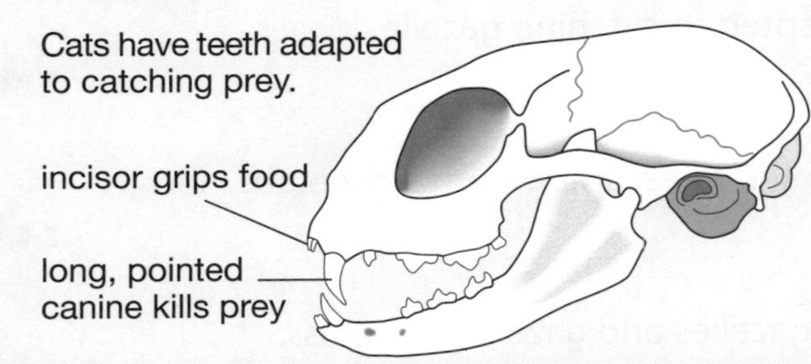

Humming birds have long beaks so they can reach the nectar in the flower.

FOOD CHAINS AND FOOD WEBS

- Some animals eat plants, and some animals eat other animals. If it is a simple relationship, this can be shown as a **food chain**.
- Animals that only eat plants are called **herbivores**. Animals that eat other animals are called **carnivores** and are also **predators**. The animals they eat are called **prey**.
- Anything that eats something else is a **consumer**.
- A plant is a **producer** because it captures energy from sunlight and uses it to grow.
- Simple food chains are rare. Most feeding relationships are more complicated, with herbivores eating a range of plants, and carnivores eating a variety of animals. These feeding relationships are called food webs. Animals and plants that make a food web are called a community.

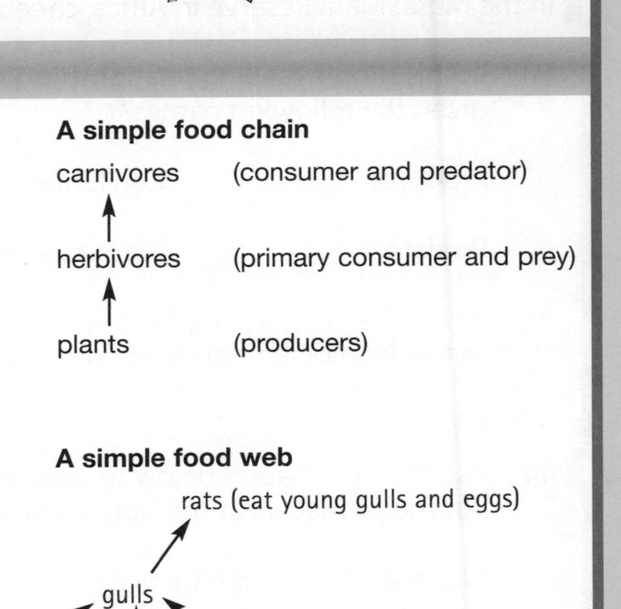

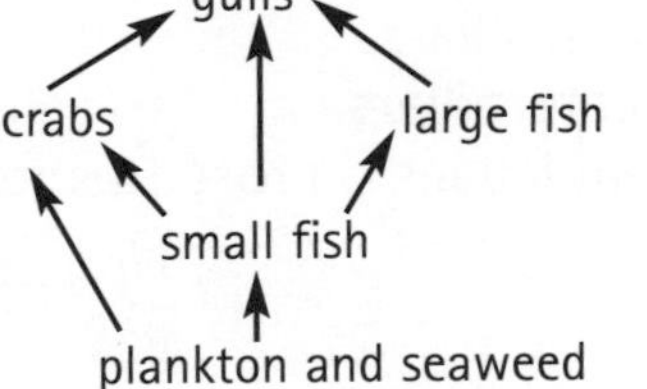

FEEDING RELATIONSHIPS

1 Join the name of the habitat to the kind of conditions to be found there.

Desert	cold and wet
Rainforest	hot and dry
Northern hills	hot and wet
Arctic tundra	cold and dry

2 marks

2 (a) Give **two** ways in which a polar bear is adapted to living in a cold habitat.

2 marks

(b) Give **two** ways in which a camel is adapted to living in the desert.

2 marks

(c) Give **two** ways in which a fish is adapted to living in the sea.

2 marks

3 (a) Describe **two** ways in which a humming bird is adapted to taking nectar from flowers that are very narrow and that are high in the trees.

2 marks

(b) Describe **two** ways in which a cheetah is adapted to catching gazelle.

2 marks

(c) Describe **two** ways in which a gazelle is adapted to escaping from a cheetah.

2 marks

4 In the Masai Mara Reserve in Africa, cheetahs eat gazelles and gazelles eat grass.

(a) In this simple feeding relationship, which organism, or organisms, could be given the following names?

Producer ______ Consumer ______ Prey ______

Predator ______ Carnivore ______ Herbivore ______

6 marks

(b) If no other animals or plants were involved, what name would you give to this kind of feeding relationship?

1 mark

5 (a) Use the information below to draw a simple food web for a garden. Put the producers at the bottom of the diagram.

Cats eat robins and blue tits.
Robins eat caterpillars.
Blue tits eat caterpillars.
Caterpillars eat leaves on rose bushes.

3 marks

TOTAL

How did you score?

9 or less – try again!
10 – 17 – nearly there!
18 – 24 – well done!

VARIATION AND CLASSIFICATION

Week 1 Thursday

What you need to know

1. Know that there is **variation** within and between **species**.
2. Know that there are patterns of variation in living things.
3. Know why there is variation.
4. Know ways to represent variation.
5. Know why **classification** is important.
6. Know about some groups of animals including **vertebrates** and **mammals**.

VARIATION

- No organism is exactly the same as another organism even if it is the same type. Slight differences in genes and in the environment make them grow to be slightly different from each other.
  Differences may include:
  - colour;
  - shape;
  - height;
  - smell;
  - weight.
- Differences can be very clear, such as your blood group. These differences are inherited from our parents.
- Other differences show a gradual **variation**, such as height or weight. These can be due to environment as well as our genes.
- Different kinds of graphs are used to represent these differences.

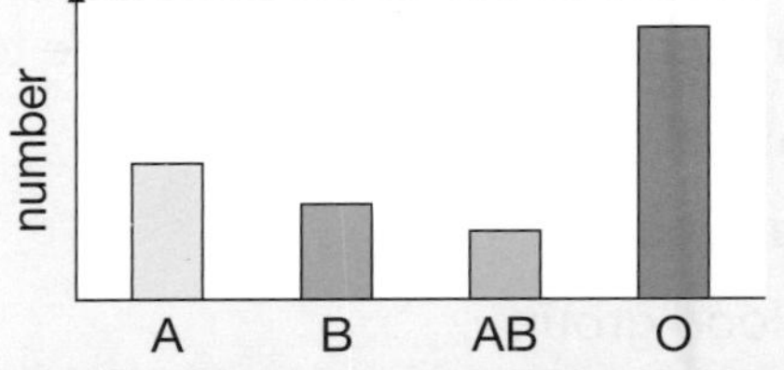

Graph showing numbers of people with certain blood groups.

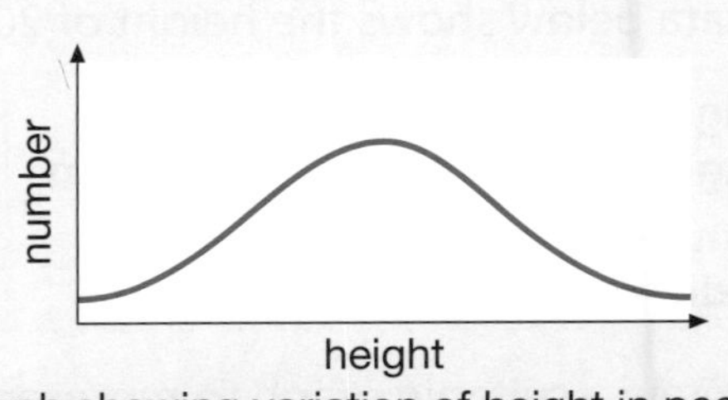

Graph showing variation of height in people.

WHY DO WE CLASSIFY ANIMALS?

- Grouping or classifying animals and plants helps us to understand how they may be related to each other. It also allows scientists to share information about animals and plants without any confusion.
- Animals are grouped depending on certain features. The table shows some features of some animal groups. There are many other kinds of animals such as worms, sponges and molluscs.

	How do they breathe?	Cold or warm blooded?	Eggs or live young?	Backbone?
Mammals	lungs	warm	live young	yes
Reptiles	lungs	cold	eggs	yes
Birds	lungs	warm	eggs	yes
Insects	network of tubes	cold	eggs	no
Fish	gills	cold	eggs	yes

VARIATION AND CLASSIFICATION

1 Put each of the animals below into the correct group.

8 marks

parrot snake blue whale human cockroach plaice crocodile flying squirrel

Mammal	Reptile	Bird	Fish	Insect

2 Put each of the animals below into one of two groups – those with backbones (vertebrates) and those without backbones (invertebrates).

human dog cat snail slug ant jellyfish whale

Backbone	No backbone

8 marks

3 Some differences between animals and plants are due to genes. Other differences are due to the environment.

Decide which of the following differences are due to genes, which are due to environment and which may be due to a mixture of both factors.

The natural colour of your hair ______________________________

How tall you are ______________________________

Your blood group ______________________________

How fast you can run ______________________________

4 marks

4 The data below shows the height of 200 female university students.

Height range	Less than 144 cm	145 to 147 cm	148 to 150 cm	151 to 153 cm	154 to 156 cm	157 to 159 cm	160 and over
Number of students	12	30	37	45	38	28	10

(a) Draw a suitable graph to represent the data.

4 marks

(b) A fashion designer designs clothes for young women who are 154 cm or taller. Use the data to estimate the number of people who might want to buy her clothes. The total number of adults in the age range is approximately 20 million.

____

2 marks

5 The data below shows the number of pupils who were right-handed and those who were left-handed.

	Left-handed	Right-handed
Number in the class	2	21

(a) Present the data in a suitable way.

2 marks

(b) An inventor has invented a computer mouse specially designed for left-handed people. Use the data above to predict how many people in the United Kingdom might be left-handed. The total number of people in the UK is approximately 56 000 000 (56 million).

______________________________ 2 marks

TOTAL

How did you score?

11 or less – try again!
12 – 21 – nearly there!
22 – 30 – well done!

ACIDS AND ALKALIS

Week 1
Friday

What you need to know

1. Know that **acids** and **alkalis** are classes of chemicals with distinct properties and uses.
2. Know what is meant by **neutralisation**.
3. Know that **indicators** are used to classify solutions as acidic, alkaline or neutral.
4. Know how to use the **pH scale** to compare the acidity and alkalinity of different solutions.

WHAT ARE ACIDS AND ALKALIS?

- Water is made from molecules of oxygen and hydrogen atoms. However, it also contains electrically charged hydrogen atoms called hydrogen ions.
- Water normally contains 1 hydrogen ion for every 10 million water molecules. If there are a higher proportion of ions than in normal water, the solution is acidic.
- When chemicals are added to water, they may react with the water so there are fewer hydrogen ions than normal. If this happens, the solution is an **alkali**.
- Although many **acids** are not normally harmful (e.g. citric acid), some acids and alkalis can be very hazardous because they are very reactive. They are also very useful substances.

Acids	Alkalis
hydrochloric acid	sodium hydroxide
sulphuric acid	bleach
vinegar	paint stripper
citric acid	many household cleaners

This car battery contains sulphuric acid.

SULPHURIC ACID

BLEACH

Bleach is a very strong alkali. It must be handled with care.

NEUTRALISATION AND PH

- 'pH' means the proportion of hydrogen ions in the water.
- Normally water has 10 000 000 times more water molecules than hydrogen ions. It has a pH of '7'. Count the zeros in the number above to see where the 7 comes from!
- An acid with a pH of 5, has 100 000 times more water molecules than hydrogen ions.
- For an alkali with a pH of 10, the proportion is 10 000 000 000 water molecules to 1 hydrogen ion.
- By mixing an alkali with an acid in the right proportions, it is possible to get the proportion of ions to be the same as in normal water. This is called **neutralisation**.

To find out how acidic or alkaline a liquid is, we use **indicator** paper (litmus paper) or an indicator liquid. The colour of the indicator shows us the acidity or alkalinity.

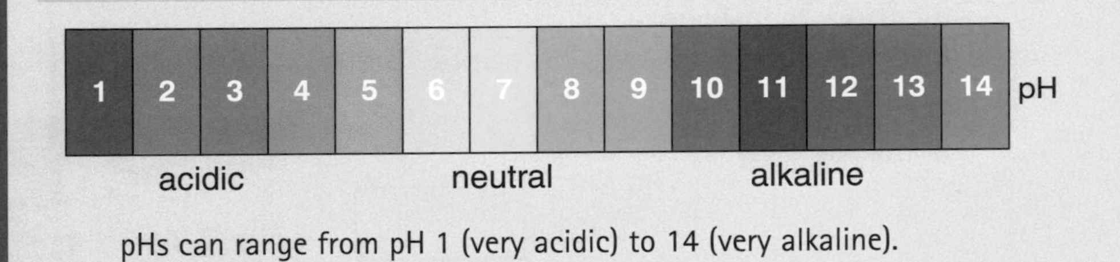

pHs can range from pH 1 (very acidic) to 14 (very alkaline).

ACIDS AND ALKALIS

1 List **three** acidic substances.

3 marks

2 List **three** alkaline substances.

3 marks

3 Some solutions were tested and were found to have the following pH values.
Decide whether each one is a strong alkali, a weak alkali, neutral, a weak acid or a strong acid.

pH 13 pH 7.3 pH 2 pH 7 pH 6.6

5 marks

4 Neutral water has a pH of 7. It has 10 000 000 times more water molecules than hydrogen ions.

What are the proportions of water molecules to hydrogen ions in these solutions?

(a) A solution of bleach with a pH of 8

1 mark

(b) A solution of sulphuric acid with a pH of 4

1 mark

5 Look at the three solutions below. Use the pH scale to decide what their pH is.

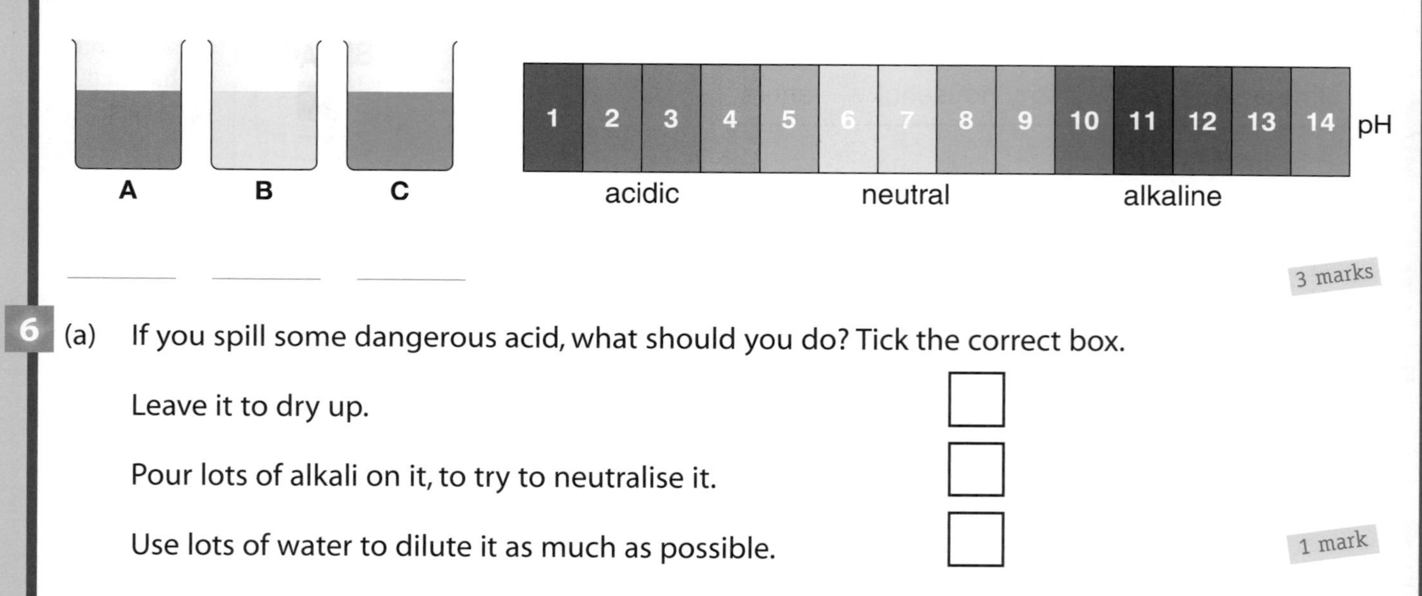

3 marks

6 (a) If you spill some dangerous acid, what should you do? Tick the correct box.

Leave it to dry up. ☐

Pour lots of alkali on it, to try to neutralise it. ☐

Use lots of water to dilute it as much as possible. ☐

1 mark

(b) Explain the reasons behind your choice of answer.

1 mark

TOTAL

How did you score?
7 or less – try again!
8 – 13 – nearly there!
14 – 18 – well done!

SIMPLE CHEMICAL REACTIONS

What you need to know

1. Know that **chemical change** results in new substances that are different from the ones from which they were made.
2. Know how to use word equations as shorthand descriptions of reactions.
3. Know that burning is a chemical reaction involving air or **oxygen**.
4. Know some simple chemical reactions of acids in which a **gas** is made.

CHEMICAL REACTIONS

- A **chemical reaction** occurs when atoms are reorganised so that they bond to different atoms. At the end of a reaction, the substances may look and behave in very different ways from how they started.

Example: When hydrogen reacts with **oxygen**, the atoms in the hydrogen molecules break apart, and the atoms in the oxygen molecules also break apart. The atoms then re-bond to make water molecules (H_2O). This reaction can be shown in a word equation:

hydrogen + oxygen → water

Generally a reaction is described as:

reactants → products
reaction

REVERSIBLE AND IRREVERSIBLE REACTIONS

- Some reactions go only one way, whereas others can go in both directions – forwards and backwards.

	Reversible reactions	Irreversible reactions
Energy change	Little amount of energy is given out or taken in.	Large amount of energy is released or taken in.
Loss of material	Atoms do not escape.	Some atoms may escape as **gas.**
Notes	Atoms could easily go back to the way they started.	Not possible to gather the substances back together.
Example	Under the right conditions, hydrogen and nitrogen react to make ammonia. The ammonia can easily become nitrogen and hydrogen again.	Burning of a fuel in air. Large amounts of energy are released and atoms escape as gas.

IMPORTANT REACTIONS

Combustion

hydrocarbon + oxygen → carbon dioxide + water (e.g. methane)

or if there is not enough oxygen to burn the fuel fully

hydrocarbon + oxygen → carbon dioxide + carbon monoxide + water

Producing a gas from a reaction

calcium carbonate + hydrochloric acid → calcium chloride + water + carbon dioxide
(marble or chalk)

- Carbonates all have a group containing 1 carbon + 3 oxygen atoms. This is written as CO_3.
- Examples of carbonates are magnesium carbonate and calcium carbonate.
- All carbonates react with acids to release carbon dioxide gas.

SIMPLE CHEMICAL REACTIONS

1 Describe **one** sign that a chemical reaction has happened.

1 mark

2 Describe **two** signs that a chemical reaction is happening.

2 marks

3 The way that marble or chalk (calcium carbonate) reacts with acid can be shown by this word equation:

calcium carbonate + hydrochloric acid → calcium chloride + water + carbon dioxide (gas)

(a) List the reactants in the above reaction.

2 marks

(b) List the products in the above reaction.

3 marks

(c) Write a word equation for the reaction of **magnesium** carbonate with hydrochloric acid.

3 marks

(d) Explain why this reaction is **irreversible**.

2 marks

4 Under certain conditions, nitrogen and hydrogen react to make ammonia.

(a) Write a word equation to represent this reaction.

3 marks

(b) The reaction can easily go the other way. Write a word equation for this reverse reaction.

3 marks

5 Sodium reacts with water to produce sodium hydroxide and hydrogen. This can be demonstrated by placing a small amount of sodium in a large bath of water.

(a) Write a word equation to represent this reaction.

4 marks

(b) Describe how we can be sure that:

(i) a gas is being produced by the reaction.

1 mark

(ii) the gas being produced is hydrogen.

1 mark

TOTAL

How did you score?

10 or less – try again!
11 – 19 – nearly there!
20 – 25 – well done!

PARTICLE MODEL OF MATTER

Week 2 Tuesday

What you need to know

1. Know the particle model can be used to explain differences between **solids, liquids** and **gases.**
2. Know how experimental evidence supports theories and models about solids, liquids and gases.

STATES OF MATTER

- There are three states of matter: **solid**, **liquid** and **gas.** Gases and liquids are fluids.

	Solid	Liquid	Gas
Does it take up the shape of the container it is in?	no	yes	yes
Can it be compressed?	no	no	yes

- To explain the behaviour of solids, liquids and gases we can think of particles. Particles could be single atoms, small molecules, or large molecules – it doesn't matter.

	Solids	Liquids	Gases
How close together are the particles?	close	close	far apart
How strong are the bonds between particles?	strong	weak	almost zero
How are the particles arranged?	can be regular	irregular	irregular
How do the particles move?	vibrating in fixed place	moving round each other	travelling quickly in straight lines — until they bounce off something

EXPLANATIONS FOR WHAT WE OBSERVE

Gases can be compressed

Particles in a gas are a long way from each other. Therefore, they can be forced closer together.

Gases exert a pressure

Gases are made of particles that are moving at high speed. When they hit something they give it a push. Because there are many particles, it makes a steady pressure.

In hot gases, particles move faster, hitting things harder, and making the pressure greater.

Gases and liquids can diffuse

In gases and liquids the particles continuously move. Two fluids will mix just because of this movement.

It takes energy to melt solids or evaporate liquids

The strong bonds between the particles have to be broken. This takes heat energy.

PARTICLE MODEL OF MATTER

1 Give **one** similarity between a solid and a liquid.

1 mark

2 Give **one** difference between a solid and a liquid.

1 mark

3 Give **one** similarity between a liquid and a gas.

1 mark

4 Give **one** difference between a liquid and a gas.

1 mark

5 What is the name given to the changes below?

(a) Ice changing to liquid water. 1 mark

(b) Liquid water changing to steam. 1 mark

(c) Liquid water changing to ice. 1 mark

(d) Steam changing to liquid water. 1 mark

6 Explain why a liquid is very difficult to compress, but a gas can be easily compressed.

2 marks

7 Use the particle theory of matter to explain the following.

(a) An inflated balloon will get smaller when placed in a refrigerator.

2 marks

(b) Placing an aerosol can on a bonfire is very dangerous.

2 marks

(c) Solids and liquids usually expand as they get warmer.

2 marks

8 A thermometer has a large bulb of liquid at the bottom and a narrow tube.
As the temperature rises, the liquid expands and moves along the tube.

large bulb of mercury
column of mercury
narrow tube
35 36 37 38 39 40 41 42 °C

(a) Explain the advantage of having a very narrow tube compared to the large bulb.

2 marks

(b) Describe any problems that a very narrow tube may cause.

2 marks

TOTAL

How did you score?
9 or less – try again!
10 – 14 – nearly there!
15 – 20 – well done!

SOLUTIONS

Week 2
Wednesday

What you need to know

1. Know about dissolving and the separation of the components of a solution and relate this to particle theory.
2. Know how to apply the particle model of solids, liquids and gases in a range of contexts.
3. Know how to distinguish between a 'pure' substance and a **mixture**.

WHAT IS A SOLUTION?

- A solution is formed when a gas, liquid or solid dissolves in a liquid.
- The substance that dissolves in the liquid is called the **solute**.
- The liquid which dissolves the substances is called the **solvent**.
- The particles of solute spread out throughout the solvent so they cannot be seen.
- The particles in the solvent are as small as the particles of liquid, so you cannot filter a solution to separate it into its different parts.
- A **saturated** solution has as much solute dissolved in the solvent as possible.
- If a substance will not dissolve into a solvent, it is **insoluble**. A substance that is insoluble in one solvent might dissolve in another.
- **Solubility** is a measure of how easy it is to dissolve a solute into a solvent. Temperature can affect the solubility of a solute.

HOW CAN WE SEPARATE A SOLUTION?

- Three ways to separate a solution are:
  - chromatography;
  - evaporation;
  - distillation.

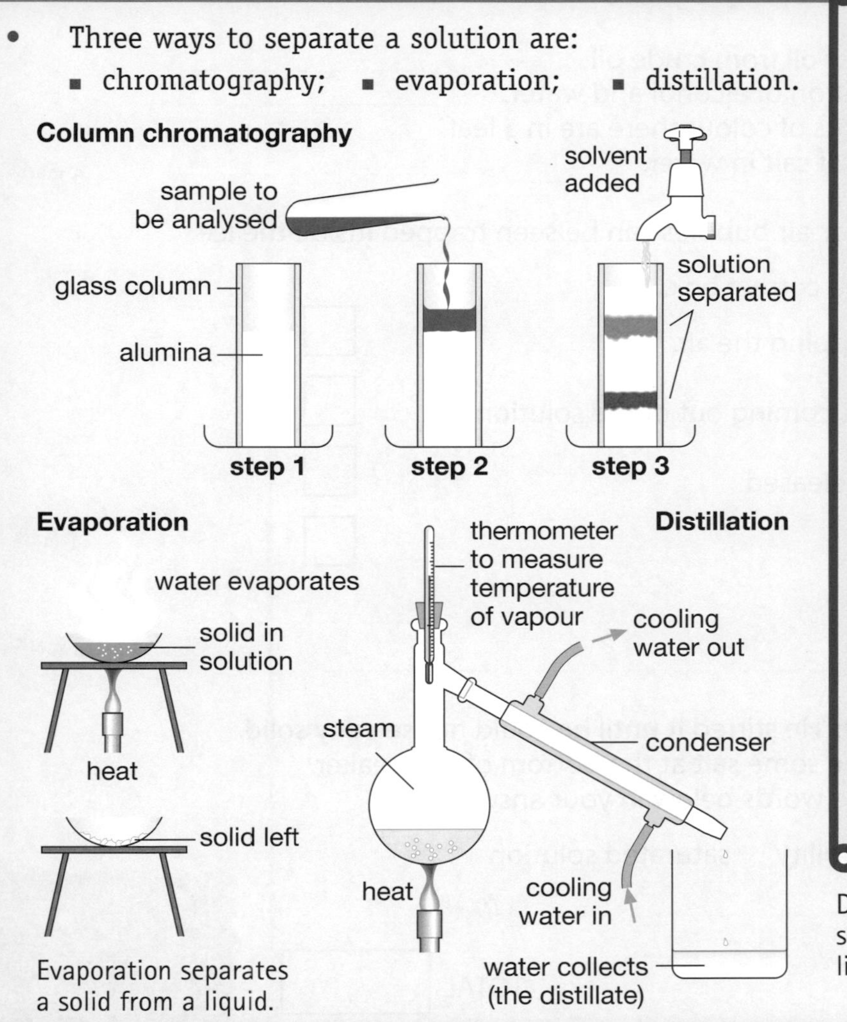

Evaporation separates a solid from a liquid.

Distillation can separate two liquids.

Remember

In a **suspension**, the particles are larger than the solute, so suspensions are cloudy.
Example: milk is cloudy because small particles of fat are suspended in the water.

A pure substance contains only one sort of particle, but it may contain different types of **atoms**.
Example: pure water contains only water molecules, but these are made from oxygen and hydrogen atoms.

A **mixture** contains a variety of substances that can be separated without using a chemical reaction.
Example: iron filings and sand could be separated using a magnet.

SOLUTIONS

1 A spoonful of sugar is added to some water so that it dissolves.

(a) What is the solvent? ______ 1 mark

(b) What is the solute? ______ 1 mark

2 When decorating, paint can be removed from a paintbrush by placing the brush in 'white spirit'.

(a) What is the solvent? ______ 1 mark

(b) What is the solute? ______ 1 mark

3 What name is given to something that will not dissolve in water?

______ 1 mark

4 Using the idea of particles, explain why suspensions are cloudy, but solutions are not cloudy.

______ 1 mark

5 The label on a carton of milk says that it contains 'Pure Milk'. From a chemist's point of view, is that statement correct? Explain your answer.

______ 2 marks

6 Chromatography, evaporation and distillation are ways to separate solutions. Which method would you use for the situations below?

A Finding out how many colours of ink are actually used to make black ink. ______

B Separating different fractions of oil from crude oil. ______

C Separating alcohol from a solution of alcohol and water. ______

D Finding out how many pigments of colour there are in a leaf. ______

E Obtaining salt from a solution of salt in water. ______

5 marks

7 When ice cubes are made in a freezer, air bubbles can be seen trapped inside the ice.

(a) Why does this happen? Tick the correct box.

A The water froze quickly, trapping the air. ☐

B Air dissolved in the water is coming out of the solution. ☐

C Air in suspension is being released. ☐

D Another reason. ☐

1 mark

(b) Explain your choice of answer.

______ 3 marks

8 Bill added salt to some boiling water. He stirred it until he could not see any solid. When the water cooled, he could see some salt at the bottom of the beaker. Explain what had happened. Use the words below in your answer:

solute solvent solution solubility saturated solution

______ 3 marks

______

TOTAL ☐

How did you score?

9 or less – try again!
10 – 14 – nearly there!
15 – 20 – well done!

ENERGY RESOURCES

Week 2 Thursday

What you need to know

1. Know that the Sun is the ultimate source of most of the Earth's **energy** resources.
2. Know about energy resources for living things: food for people and sunlight for plants.
3. Know the nature and origin of **fossil fuels**.
4. Know that fuels are convenient and valuable sources of energy.
5. Know about renewable sources of energy.
6. Know that the use of renewable sources of energy and fuels have implications for the environment.

WHERE DOES OUR ENERGY COME FROM?

- Almost all the **energy** we use originally arrived on Earth as sunlight.
- The energy from sunlight is captured by plants and used by them to grow.
- Animals eat the plants and with them the chemical energy that is stored in them.
- Millions of years ago, when some plants and animals died, they got trapped and instead of just decaying, they produced the **fossil fuels** we use today.
- Some energy we use cannot be traced back to sunlight. Examples are:
  - nuclear energy;
  - energy we get from the hot interior of the Earth;
  - energy from tides.

WHAT IS A FUEL?

- A fuel is a substance that can be burnt to release energy as heat and light.
- Fuels can be transported to where the heat is needed, so they are convenient energy sources.
- Oil, gas and coal are examples of fossil fuels.
- Whenever a fuel is burned, polluting gases are released. These gases include carbon dioxide.
- Collecting, processing and transporting the fuels can cause environmental damage, such as oil spills.

RENEWABLE SOURCES

- 'Renewable' energy sources refer to any energy source that will not run out. However, most of these sources still rely on energy from sunlight.

  Examples are:
  - wind;
  - waves;
  - tides;
  - hydroelectricity (from dams);
  - geothermal energy (heat energy from inside the Earth);
  - biomass (growing plants for fuel).
- All of these energy sources affect the environment, by being unsightly and by affecting local ecosystems. The only long-term solution is for us to use less energy. Living in homes that are slightly cooler could save a lot of energy.

Windfarms are one way to provide renewable energy.

ENERGY RESOURCES

1 Name **three** fossil fuels.

(i) ______________________

(ii) ______________________

(iii) ______________________

3 marks

2 Name **three** 'renewable' sources of energy.

(i) ______________________

(ii) ______________________

(iii) ______________________

3 marks

3 Name the gas that is released when a fuel is burned.

____

1 mark

4 Where does the majority of the energy we use come from?

____

2 marks

5 Explain why using fossil fuels can cause problems.

____

2 marks

6 Explain why using renewable sources of energy can cause problems.

____

2 marks

7 Power stations are often built a long way from cities where the electrical energy is needed.

(a) What are the benefits of building them far away?

____

2 marks

(b) What are the problems of building them far away?

____

2 marks

8 List **three** ways to reduce our demand for energy.

____

____

____

3 marks

TOTAL

How did you score?

9 or less – try again!
10 – 14 – nearly there!
15 – 20 – well done!

ELECTRICAL CIRCUITS

Week 2 Friday

What you need to know

1. Know how to design electrical circuits in which current flow is controlled.
2. Know that an electric current requires a complete circuit to flow.
3. Know the relationship between **current** and voltage for resistors and bulbs.
4. Know what is meant by **resistance**.
5. Know that electricity can be hazardous.
6. Know how to use electric current and energy transfer to explain the working of circuits.

CONTROLLING ELECTRICAL CURRENT

- An electric current is a flow of charged particles. To be able to move, the charged particles need to be in an electrical conductor.
- The conductor must form a complete circuit.
- An electric **current** cannot flow through an electrical **insulator**.
- The charged particles carry electrical energy to components in the circuit.

VOLTAGE AND RESISTANCE

- The 'voltage' across an electrical component indicates the amount of energy the component is adding to, or taking from, the current.
- Components with a high **resistance** turn more electrical energy into heat than components with a low resistance, assuming the electrical current is the same.
- Components with a high resistance keep the current in a circuit lower than components with a low resistance, assuming the voltage stays the same.
- When resistors become hot, their resistance increases.
- An electric shock can be very dangerous because it can damage the heart, skin, nervous system and the brain.

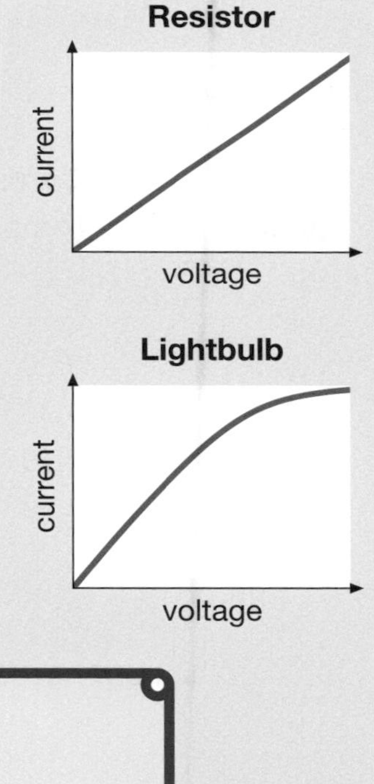

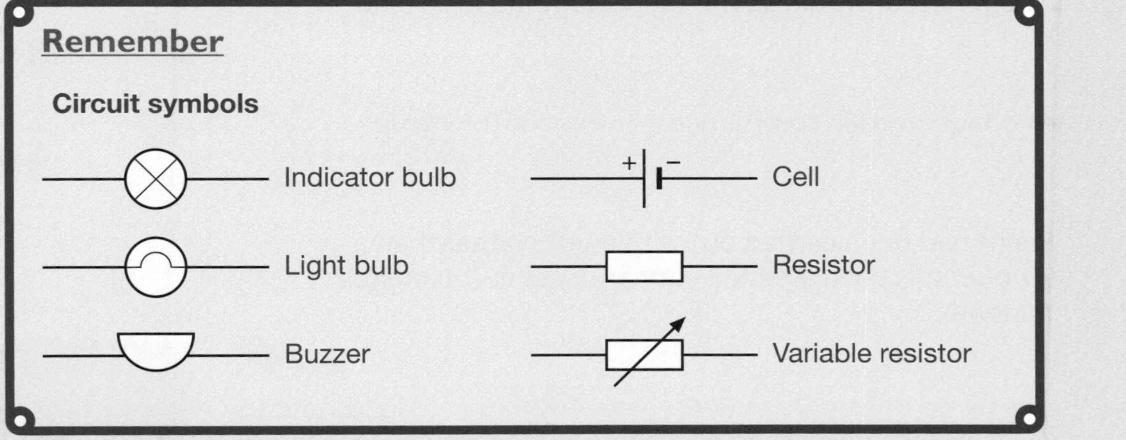

ELECTRICAL CIRCUITS

1 Which components are represented by these symbols?

3 marks

2 The circuits below were suggested by a pupil as a way to make a bulb light. None of them work. State what is wrong with each circuit, and explain why this fault stops the circuit from working.

3 marks

3 The data below was collected using the circuit shown.

Voltage (Volts)	Current (Amperes)
0	0
2.0	0.10
4.0	0.20
6.0	0.30
8.0	0.40
10.0	0.50

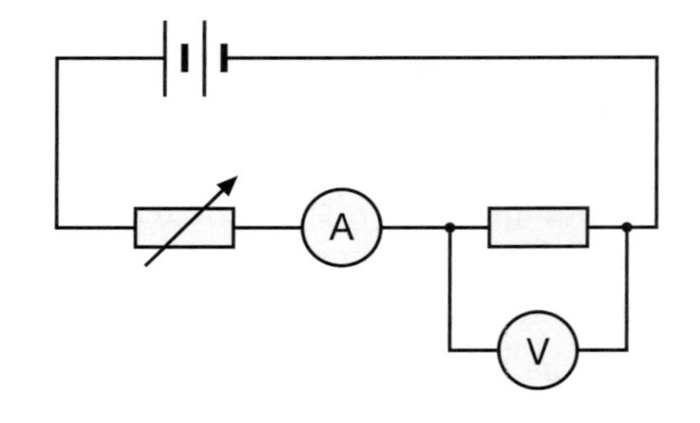

(a) Plot a graph of the data.

2 marks

(b) Estimate the current that would flow if the voltage was 12 Volts.

1 mark

(c) Estimate the voltage needed to produce a current of 0.15 Amps.

1 mark

(d) If the experiment had been carried out with a bulb rather than a resistor, how would this have affected your answers to (b) and (c)? Explain your answer.

2 marks

TOTAL

How did you score?

5 or less – try again!
6 – 8 – nearly there!
9 – 12 – well done!

FORCES AND THEIR EFFECTS

Week 3 Monday

What you need to know

1. Know what is meant by **force** and how it is measured.
2. Know what balanced and unbalanced forces are and be able to recognise them.
3. Know how forces can change motion.
4. Know why **friction** happens.
5. Know about air resistance, **upthrust** and **weight** and describe situations in which these forces act.
6. Know the difference between mass and weight.
7. Know the concept of speed.

BALANCED AND UNBALANCED FORCES

- The strength of a **force** is measured in **Newtons**.
- A **forcemeter** is used to measure the strength of a force.
- Two forces of equal strength, acting in opposite directions, are called balanced forces.

4 N ← □ → 4 N

These forces are in balance, so there is no change to the movement of the object.

- A force that has no force to balance it is called an unbalanced force.

A simple forcemeter

spring inside

NEWTONS

graduated scale

HOW DO FORCES AFFECT OBJECTS?

- A moving object will travel in a straight line at a constant speed *unless* an unbalanced force acts on it.
- An unbalanced force can change the direction in which the object is travelling. An unbalanced force can change the speed of the object.
- A stationary object may have large balanced forces acting on the object. A stationary object will stay still unless an unbalanced force acts on it.
- An unbalanced force can make an object spin faster or slower.

IMPORTANT FORCES

- Air resistance opposes the movement of any object moving through air, but it only acts when an object is moving.
- **Friction** is caused by surfaces rubbing together and it opposes movement. Frictional forces can act when an object is still, matching a force that is trying to move it.
- **Gravity** acts on any object with mass. The more mass an object has, the larger the pull of gravity. We call this pull the **weight** of the object.
- An object that is floating has balanced forces acting on it. The weight of the object is matched by the **upthrust** from the water.
- An object that is stretched is said to be 'under tension'.

Remember

Weight is a force and is measured in Newtons.
Mass is NOT a force and is measured in kilograms.

Average speed = distance travelled /time taken.
It is measured in kilometres per hour or metres per second.

FORCES AND THEIR EFFECTS

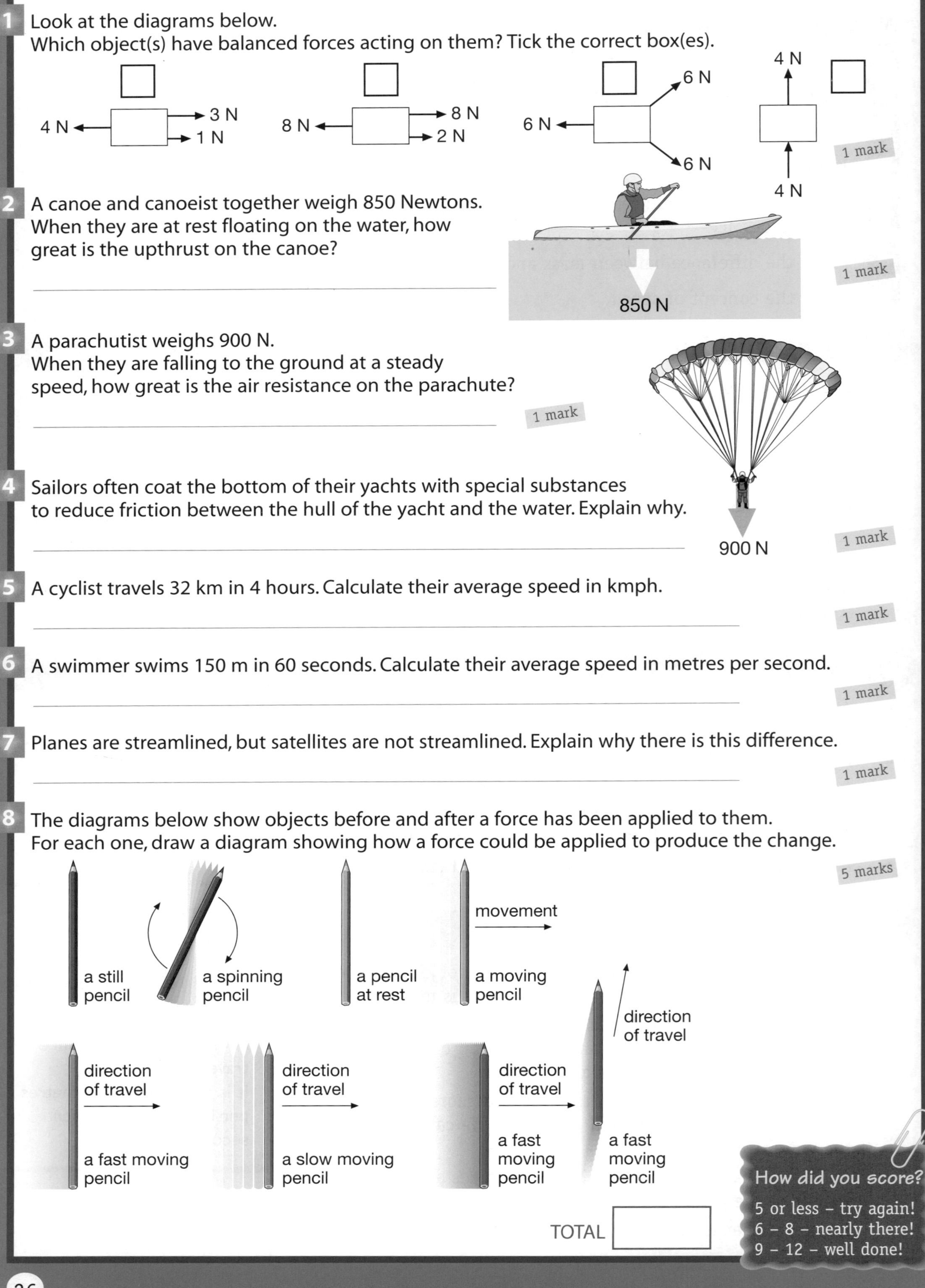

1 Look at the diagrams below.
Which object(s) have balanced forces acting on them? Tick the correct box(es).

1 mark

2 A canoe and canoeist together weigh 850 Newtons. When they are at rest floating on the water, how great is the upthrust on the canoe?

1 mark

3 A parachutist weighs 900 N.
When they are falling to the ground at a steady speed, how great is the air resistance on the parachute?

1 mark

4 Sailors often coat the bottom of their yachts with special substances to reduce friction between the hull of the yacht and the water. Explain why.

1 mark

5 A cyclist travels 32 km in 4 hours. Calculate their average speed in kmph.

1 mark

6 A swimmer swims 150 m in 60 seconds. Calculate their average speed in metres per second.

1 mark

7 Planes are streamlined, but satellites are not streamlined. Explain why there is this difference.

1 mark

8 The diagrams below show objects before and after a force has been applied to them.
For each one, draw a diagram showing how a force could be applied to produce the change.

5 marks

TOTAL

How did you score?
5 or less – try again!
6 – 8 – nearly there!
9 – 12 – well done!

THE SOLAR SYSTEM AND BEYOND

Week 3 Tuesday

What you need to know

1. Know why and how the Sun, Earth and Moon move relative to each other, and their relative sizes.
2. Know that the Sun is the nearest star to the Earth.
3. Know how to explain **eclipses** and the seasons.
4. Know that planets and satellites are seen by reflected light and that the Sun, as a star, emits light.

EARTH, MOON AND SUN

- The Sun's diameter is approximately 110 times larger than the Earth's diameter.
- The Earth passes around the Sun once every 365.25 days.
- The Sun is the nearest star to the Earth.
- As the Earth moves around the Sun, it revolves on its axis once every 24 hours. The path it follows around the Sun is an ellipse (not a circle).
- The Earth's diameter is approximately four times larger than the Moon's diameter. It orbits the Earth once every 28 days.
- As the Moon moves around the Earth, it revolves on its axis once every 28 days. The path the Moon follows around the Earth is an ellipse (not a circle).
- The force holding the Sun, Earth and Moon together is **gravity**.

Remember
Stars emit light, but planets and satellites (including the Moon) do not emit light. We only see them because they reflect sunlight towards us.

ECLIPSES

- When the Moon passes between the Earth and the Sun, the Moon casts a shadow onto the Earth. People who are standing where the shadow falls see a solar eclipse.
- When the Moon moves into the Earth's shadow, the Moon goes dark. People on the side of the Earth facing the Moon see a lunar eclipse.

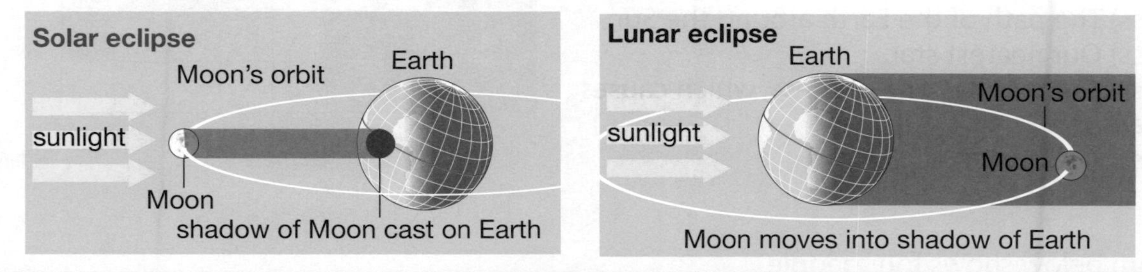

SEASONS

The axis of the Earth is tilted, so that at certain times of year, the South Pole faces the Sun, whilst the North Pole faces away. Six months later the situation is reversed, because the Earth has moved halfway around the Sun.
The area that faces the Sun, has longer days, and receives more sunlight than the area that faces away. The area that faces towards the Sun experiences summer. Meanwhile the area that faces away experiences winter. Six months later, the situation is reversed.

THE SOLAR SYSTEM AND BEYOND

1 Imagine you are making a model of the solar system. You choose a small ball, 1 cm in diameter, to represent the Moon.

(a) To the same scale, how large would the diameter of the model of the Earth be?

____ 1 mark

(b) To the same scale, how large would the diameter of the model of the Sun be?

____ 1 mark

2 Explain why it is more common for us to see a lunar eclipse than a solar eclipse.

____ 2 marks

3 The Earth has one natural satellite. What do we call it?

____ 1 mark

4 What is the name of the star that is nearest to us?

____ 1 mark

5 List these objects in order of size starting with the largest: satellite, planet, star.

____ 3 marks

6 Light from the Sun takes eight minutes to reach Earth.
It takes so long, because light travels very slowly. Tick the correct box.

True ☐ False ☐ 1 mark

7 Try this acrostic.

Clues

1 (down) The season we have when the North Pole is facing away from the Sun.
2 (across) The path of the Earth around the Sun.
3 (across) Our nearest star.
4 (across) Our axis has one of these, which causes the seasons.
5 (across) The planet we live on.

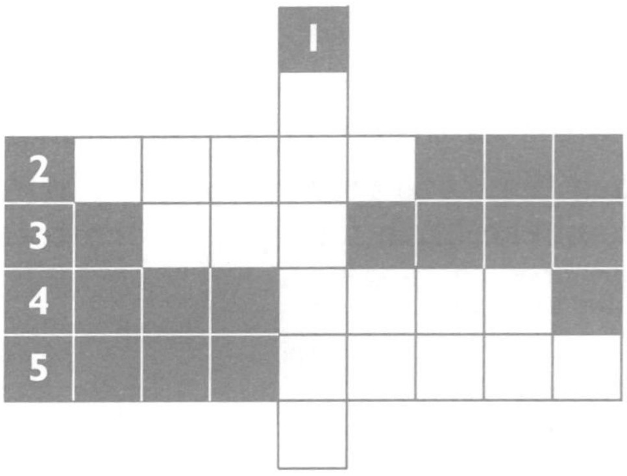

5 marks

8 The diagram below shows four people standing at different places on the Earth's surface.
Copy and complete the diagram to show which way the masses would hang.

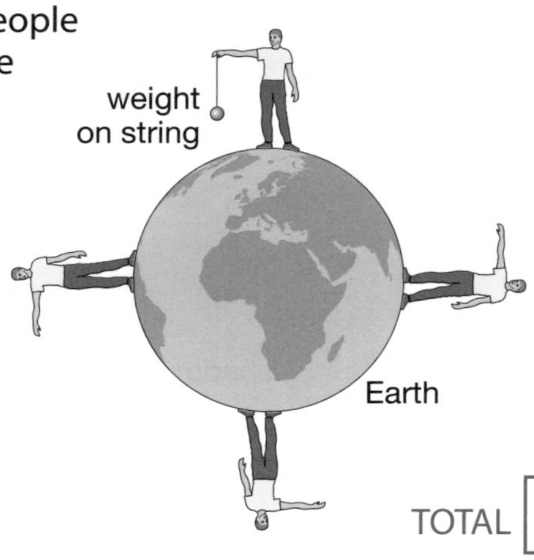

weight on string

Earth

3 marks

TOTAL

How did you score?
7 or less – try again!
8 – 13 – nearly there!
14 – 18 – well done!

FOOD AND DIGESTION

Week 3
Wednesday

What you need to know

1. Know that there are different kinds of foods.
2. Know how different food types can be combined to produce a **balanced diet**.
3. Know how food is broken down by digestion so it can be absorbed by the body and then used for **energy**, growth and repair.

EATING A BALANCE OF FOODS

- It is important that we eat a range of foods to keep us healthy. This is called a **balanced diet**.
- To have a balanced diet we must eat foods that contain:
  - carbohydrates;
  - fat;
  - protein;
  - vitamins and minerals.
- We must also eat foods that contain:
  - fibre.
- Fibre has no nutritional value, but it helps to keep the muscles in your digestive system healthy, and you are less likely to get constipation and some types of cancer.

HOW OUR BODY DEALS WITH FOOD

- The food we eat has to be broken down so that we can use it in our bodies. This process involves:
  - chewing it with our teeth;
  - mixing it with acidic digestive juices in the stomach to kill bacteria;
  - adding **enzymes** that dissolve the food.
- The nutrients can then be absorbed through the intestine wall and carried to cells around the body.
- The last process is to absorb water back into the body.

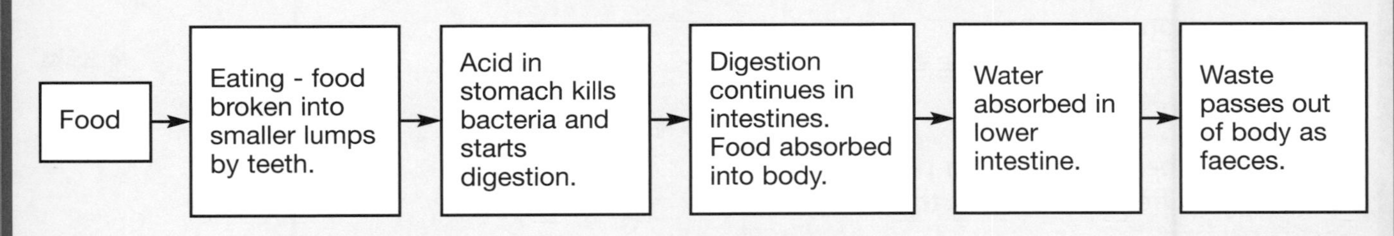

HOW OUR BODY USES THE FOOD WE EAT

- The substances we get from food allow us to:
  - make new cells so we can grow larger;
  - replace cells that die;
  - provide us with fuel to keep warm and to move;
  - produce sex cells so we can reproduce.

FOOD AND DIGESTION

1 Young people need to eat food to help them to grow. Why else is it important that they eat a balanced diet?

____

____ 2 marks

2 Older people do not need to eat to enable them to grow larger. Why is it important that they continue to eat a balanced diet?

____

____ 2 marks

3 Fibre has no nutritional value. Why is it important that we eat it?

____

____ 1 mark

4 Explain why it is important that you chew your food so that it is broken into smaller lumps before you swallow it.

____

____ 2 marks

5 Sometimes you might get diarrhoea. Which part of the digestive process is not working when this happens?

____ 1 mark

6 Some people suffer from bulimia, a disease that makes them overeat and vomit. People with this problem often have badly decayed teeth. Explain why.

____

____ 2 marks

7 Some people who suffer from cancer of the large intestine (bowel) have to have part of their intestine removed. Assuming the operation is successful, what problems might they continue to face?

____

____ 2 marks

TOTAL [   ]

How did you score?

5 or less – try again!
6 – 8 – nearly there!
9 – 12 – well done!

RESPIRATION

Week 3
Thursday

What you need to know

1. Know how **cells** are supplied with the materials they need for **respiration.**
2. Know how cells in animals and plants release **energy**.
3. Know that the process of respiration is similar in all cells.

WHY DO WE NEED TO BREATHE?

- All **cells** must respire to make **energy** from sugar to survive.
- To respire, cells must have glucose and **oxygen**.
- **Aerobic respiration** can be represented by the following equation:

glucose + oxygen → carbon dioxide + water

- Inhaling fresh air enables the body to take in **oxygen** for aerobic respiration.
- Exhaling allows the body to get rid of carbon dioxide which is poisonous.

HOW DOES OXYGEN GET TO OUR CELLS?

- Humans use lungs to breathe. These are positioned inside the ribcage, which protects them.
- When you breathe in, oxygen passes through the lining of your lungs, and is absorbed by **haemoglobin** in red blood cells.
- Your heart beats to push the blood through **arteries** around your body. The blood returns to your heart through **veins.** This is called circulation of blood.

The lungs have a very delicate structure. They can be easily damaged by smoke.

RESPIRATION DURING EXERCISE

- When you exercise, more oxygen and glucose is needed by your cells, and more carbon dioxide and water needs to be removed.
- Your heart beats faster to get more blood to and from your cells.
- You breathe more deeply to get more oxygen into your blood, and to get rid of more carbon dioxide.
- Your heart is beating faster, so your pulse rate increases.

Remember

When you exhale not all of the carbon dioxide in your body comes out. However, the concentration of carbon dioxide in your blood reduces. When you inhale, the concentration of oxygen in your blood increases.

RESPIRATION

1 Label the diagram below to show the following: trachea, bronchus and lungs. 3 marks

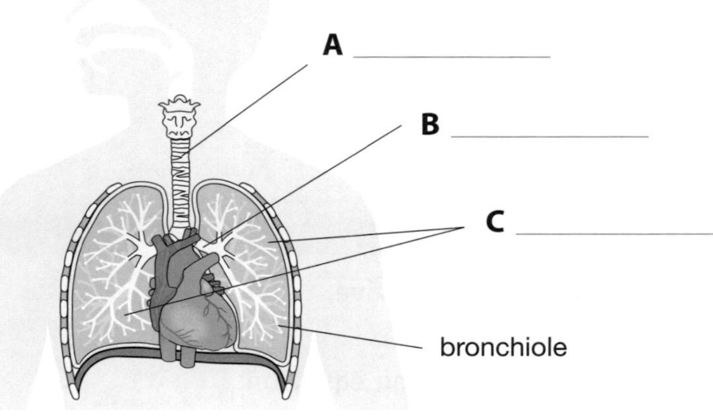

2 Complete the word equation for aerobic respiration.

glucose + ________________ → ________________ + water 2 marks

3 Which gas enters your body when you inhale (breathe in)?

______________________________ 1 mark

4 Which gas leaves your body when you exhale (breathe out)?

______________________________ 1 mark

5 'When you breathe out, you get rid of all the carbon dioxide in your body.' True or false?

______________________________ 1 mark

6 'Veins carry blood away from the heart and arteries carry it back.' True or false?

______________________________ 1 mark

7 'All plant cells respire.' True or false? ________________ 1 mark

8 (a) In which part of your body would you find **haemoglobin**?

______________________________ 1 mark

(b) What is the function of haemoglobin? ________________ 1 mark

9 When you exercise, you breathe more deeply and your heart beats faster.
Explain why your body reacts in this way.

______________________________ 2 marks

10 Smokers inhale carbon monoxide. Red blood cells absorb carbon monoxide which damages haemoglobin so that it cannot absorb oxygen.
Explain why people who smoke can appear 'out of breath'.

______________________________ 2 marks

TOTAL

How did you score?
7 or less – try again!
8 – 12 – nearly there!
13 – 16 – well done!

MICROBES AND DISEASE

Week 3
Friday

What you need to know

1. Know that **microorganisms** share the characteristics of all living things.
2. Know how microorganisms can cause infectious diseases.
3. Know how your body's defence system works and how **immunisation** can protect you against microbial infections.
4. Know that microorganisms are used to make products.

WHAT IS A MICROORGANISM?

- Some **microorganisms** consist of single cells. These include bacteria, some algae, some fungi, moulds and yeasts. They are often called germs. In the right conditions germs can reproduce rapidly.
- Microorganisms produce waste products as part of their normal life processes. These waste products can make us feel extremely ill.
- Some microorganisms, such as **viruses**, are smaller than a single cell and cannot reproduce on their own. To reproduce, a virus takes over a cell and forces the cell to make copies of the virus.

HOW CAN WE PROTECT OURSELVES?

Viruses

- When our immune system recognises a virus, it produces **antibodies**.
- In a **vaccination** or inoculation, a doctor gives us a small dose of a specially weakened microorganism. The body can practise against this one so that when the real one enters the body, the immune system can react much more quickly.

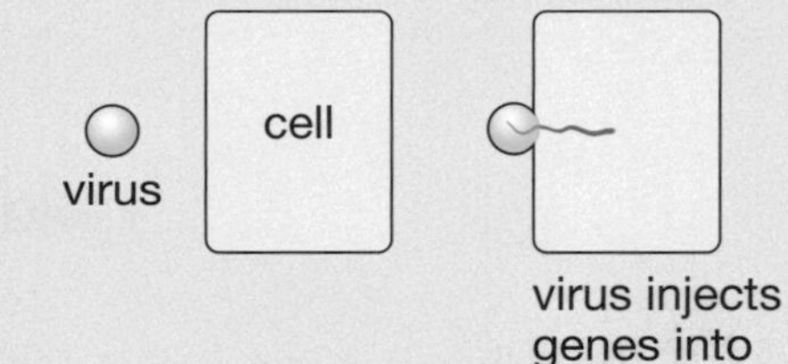

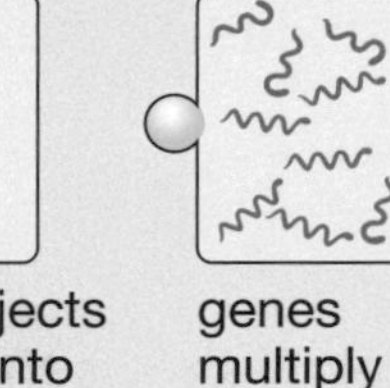

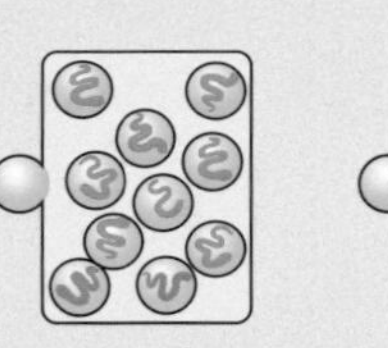

the cell bursts open and the new viruses are set free

Viruses can only reproduce inside living cells. Here a virus attacks and destroys a cell.

Bacteria

- To kill bacteria, we can use antiseptics and very high temperatures. This is called sterilisation.
- We can also use chemicals called antibiotics.
- If we are hygienic, we expose ourselves to fewer bacteria.
- We can be vaccinated against some bacteria.

Remember

- Antibiotics are not effective against a virus.
- A pathogen is a microorganism that can cause a disease.
- An infectious disease can be passed on through air or water.
- A contagious disease can only be passed on by direct contact.
- A disease which infects a large number of people is an epidemic.

USEFUL MICROBES

- Some microbes are helpful:
  - yeast is used in bread-making and brewing;
  - penicillin is an antibiotic made by a fungus;
  - microbes help our digestion;
  - microbes are used to make yoghurt.

MICROBES AND DISEASE

1 Give **one** way in which microorganisms are helpful to us.

1 mark

2 Give **one** way in which microorganisms are harmful to us.

1 mark

3 What is the name given to a disease that rapidly infects a large number of people?

1 mark

4 Describe the difference between a **contagious** disease and an **infectious** disease.

2 marks

5 Describe how a virus reproduces.

2 marks

6 Explain why our blood contains 'antibodies'.

1 mark

7 Explain why keeping food in a refrigerator makes it 'last longer'.

1 mark

8 Give **two** ways that can reduce the danger from bacteria.

2 marks

9 Explain why receiving an inoculation can prevent us from getting measles.

2 marks

10 To reproduce, a single bacteria splits in two. The table below shows the number of bacteria present after a short period of time.

Calculate the three missing values in the table.

Time (minutes)	Number
0	1
5	2
10	4
15	8
20	16
30	
60 (1 hour)	
120 (2 hours)	

3 marks

TOTAL

How did you score?

7 or less – try again!
8 – 12 – nearly there!
13 – 16 – well done!

ECOLOGICAL RELATIONSHIPS

Week 4 Monday

What you need to know

1. Know that living things within a community influence each other and are affected by the environment.
2. Know that feeding relationships can be modelled quantitatively.
3. Know that organisms can be identified and sizes of populations compared.

INTERDEPENDENCE

- Organisms that live in the same habitat form a community.
- In communities, organisms are interdependent. A change in one organism affects all the others.

If hunters killed a large number of **predators** (e.g. foxes), their **prey** (e.g. rabbits) would tend to live longer. As a result more primary producers would be eaten (e.g. grass).

REPRESENTING COMMUNITIES

- **Food chains** show feeding relationships in communities. When all of these food chains join together, they form a food web.
- A **pyramid of numbers** shows the numbers of organisms at different feeding levels in a community.
- A pyramid of biomass shows the mass of organisms at different feeding levels in a community.
- To find out the numbers of different plant species, or to see how they are distributed, biologists can use:
  - transects;
  - quadrats.
- It is important that biologists can classify plants and animals, so they are sure they are only counting those of one type.

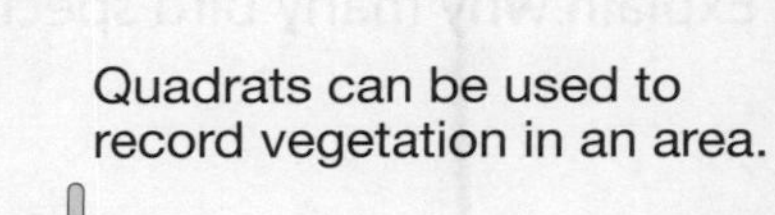

SLEEP OR MOVE?

- In winter, the amount of light energy arriving in an area reduces, so it is cold and there is less plant food to eat. As a result:
  - some animals migrate to spend the winter in a warmer place with more food;
  - some animals hibernate, so their need for energy is less;
  - seeds lie dormant in soil waiting until there is more sunlight and higher temperatures.
- To find out the number of animals, or to see how they are distributed, biologists may be able to:
  - count them directly (for large animals that are easy to spot);
  - count piles of dung (for large animals that can hide easily);
  - use mark-release and recapture (for small animals).

ECOLOGICAL RELATIONSHIPS

1 (a) In the food web shown below, identify the following:

(i) producers ______________________________

(ii) primary consumers ______________________________

(iii) predators ______________________________

(iv) carnivores ______________________________

4 marks

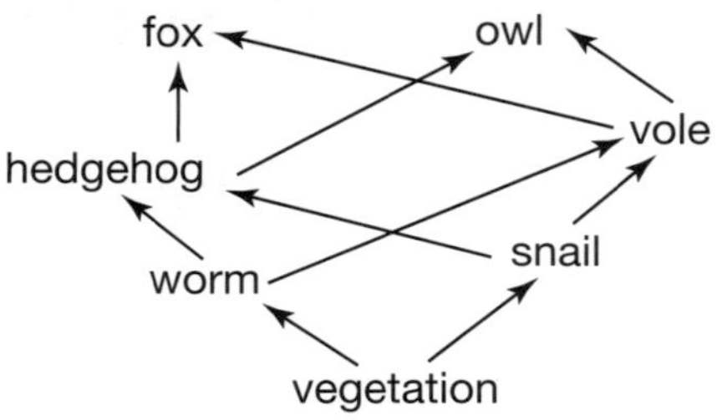

fox ← vole, fox ← hedgehog, owl ← hedgehog, owl ← vole, vole ← worm, vole ← snail, hedgehog ← worm, hedgehog ← snail, worm ← vegetation, snail ← vegetation

(b) Describe what might happen to the organisms in the community if hunters killed all the foxes.

____

2 marks

(c) Describe what might happen to the organisms in the community if a disease meant that snails could no longer breed.

____

2 marks

2 Explain why many bird species migrate South in the autumn and North in the spring.

____

2 marks

3 Explain why some animals hibernate in winter.

____

2 marks

4 Two typical pyramids of numbers are shown here. One is for summer and one for winter.

Summer

Winter

Suggest why there are the following differences between the pyramids.

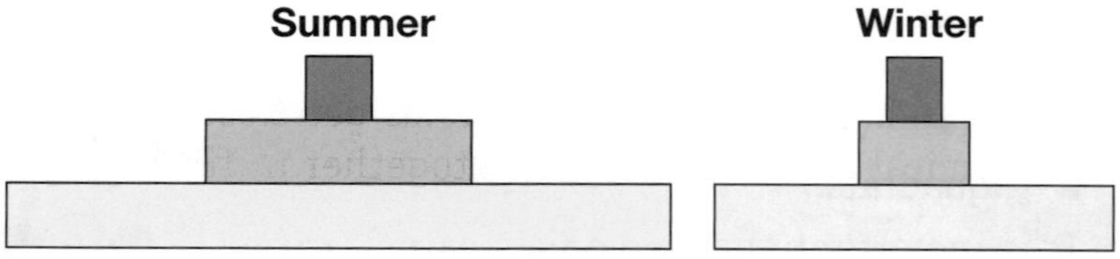

(a) There are fewer producers in winter than in summer.

____

2 marks

(b) There are fewer primary consumers in winter than in summer.

____

2 marks

(c) The number of predators is almost the same, even though they have little to eat.

____

2 marks

5 Describe **one** way of estimating the proportions of different types of vegetation in a habitat.

____

2 marks

TOTAL

How did you score?

9 or less – try again!
10 – 14 – nearly there!
15 – 20 – well done!

ATOMS AND ELEMENTS

What you need to know

1. Know that each **element** is composed of only one sort of **atom**.
2. Know the characteristics of some elements.
3. Know how to describe what happens when elements combine.
4. Know that the huge range of materials is made from a relatively small number of elements.

ATOMS AND ELEMENTS

- All matter is made of **atoms**. 92 kinds of atoms occur naturally but larger atoms can be made in nuclear reactors.
- Substances made from only one kind of atom are called **elements**.
  Oxygen, hydrogen and carbon are examples of elements.
- Each element has a unique set of characteristics:
  - some elements are very reactive (hydrogen, potassium and chlorine);
  - other elements do not react easily if at all (helium);
  - some elements are gases at room temperature and others are solids;
  - some elements conduct electricity and others do not.

LINKING ATOMS

- By linking atoms together, it is possible to make thousands of different kinds of materials.
- Each of these materials has its own characteristics such as strength, density and colour.
- The characteristics of the material can be very different from the characteristics of the elements that make it.

> Water is made from hydrogen and oxygen. Hydrogen is explosive and oxygen is needed for substances to burn, but together they make a substance that is used to put out fires.

- When elements combine, the atoms get close to each other and bond together in a chemical reaction. They link together in fixed proportions to make a **compound**.
- Sometimes millions of atoms can bond in a very regular arrangement. Sodium and chlorine atoms bond in this way to make salt crystals.

Crystal lattice

- Plastics are made up of long molecules of bonded carbon and hydrogen atoms.

Polythene molecule

- In other materials, only a few atoms link together. A water molecule is made from just one oxygen atom bonded to two hydrogen atoms.

Water molecules

ATOMS AND ELEMENTS

1 Complete the table below to show which are elements and which are not elements. One is done for you.

	Element	Not an element
oxygen	yes	
water		
salt		
air		
hydrogen		
plastic		

5 marks

2 Complete the table below to show characteristics of the elements listed.

	oxygen	hydrogen	helium	gold
gas at room temperature				
solid at room temperature				
metal				
explosive				

4 marks

3 Complete the table below to show characteristics of the materials listed.

	wood	expanded polystyrene	paper	glass
flammable				
less dense than water				
transparent				

4 marks

4 Complete the following sentence:

For atoms to link together to become compounds they must ______________________

____ 2 marks

5 Below are some chemical symbols of elements and some names of elements. Join the element to the correct chemical symbol.

C	lead
H	chlorine
He	oxygen
O	helium
Cl	nitrogen
N	carbon
Pb	hydrogen

7 marks

6 Explain the meaning of H_2O, the chemical formula for water.

____ 2 marks

TOTAL

How did you score?

9 or less – try again!
10 – 17 – nearly there!
18 – 24 – well done!

COMPOUNDS AND MIXTURES

Week 4
Wednesday

What you need to know

1. Know the difference between **elements** and **compounds**.
2. Know that **chemical change** is a process in which **atoms** join together in new ways.
3. Know how elements and compounds are represented by symbols and **formulae.**
4. Know the difference between compounds and **mixtures.**
5. Know the difference between chemical reactions in which new compounds are formed and the formation of mixtures.

ELEMENTS AND COMPOUNDS

- **Atoms** are the building blocks of all materials.
  Atoms can link together to make compounds.
- **Compounds** are substances formed by **elements** combining together in fixed proportions.
- Formation of a compound involves a **chemical reaction.** A compound may have very different characteristics from the elements that made it. The elements in compounds cannot be separated by physical means. There must be a chemical reaction.
- A **molecule** is the smallest part of a compound that can take part in a chemical reaction.
- Not all compounds are molecules. For example: salt is a compound, but it has a crystalline structure, not a molecular structure.

SYMBOLS AND FORMULAE

- Common chemical symbols you should be familiar with include:

He	helium	Na	sodium	H	hydrogen
O	oxygen	C	carbon	Cl	chlorine

- Common chemical **formulae** you should be familiar with include:

NaCl	sodium chloride, known as common salt
H_2	a single hydrogen molecule, made of two hydrogen atoms
O_2	a single oxygen molecule, made of two oxygen atoms
H_2O	a single water molecule
$2H_2O$	two water molecules
CO_2	carbon dioxide

REACTING AND MIXING

Reacting

- A word equation shows the names of the compounds or elements involved in a reaction.

  hydrogen + oxygen → water

- Using symbols we can show the process in greater detail.

  $2H_2 + O_2 \rightarrow 2H_2O$

Here two hydrogen molecules react with an oxygen molecule to make two water molecules. The hydrogen and oxygen are elements. Water is a compound because it is made from two elements.

Mixing

- To say how to mix something properly, we do not have to use chemical symbols.
  Instead we might mix things by weight, or by size.

  mixing normal concrete: 1 part cement to 2 parts of sand to 4 parts of gravel

COMPOUNDS AND MIXTURES

1 Give the symbols for the following elements:

(a) carbon ______ 1 mark

(b) oxygen ______ 1 mark

(c) hydrogen ______ 1 mark

2 Give the formulae for these compounds:

(a) common salt ______ 1 mark

(b) water ______ 1 mark

(c) carbon dioxide ______ 1 mark

3 Describe the difference between an **element** and a **compound**.

______ 2 marks

4 Describe the difference between a **compound** and a **mixture**.

______ 2 marks

5 A sample of sand contains grit and salt. To separate the salt from the grit, water can be added to dissolve the salt. The solution can be poured off and allowed to evaporate, leaving the salt behind.

(a) Is sand a mixture or a compound? ______ 1 mark

(b) Explain your answer. ______ 1 mark

6 To make strong concrete you use 1 part cement to 2 parts of sand to 1 part of gravel.

(a) Is concrete a mixture or a compound? ______ 1 mark

(b) Explain your answer. ______ 1 mark

7 Charcoal is a porous form of carbon. It can be made from wood or coconut shells. When it is burnt in oxygen it produces carbon dioxide.

(a) Write a word equation to describe the reaction.

______ 2 marks

(b) Identify which substances are elements and which are compounds.

Elements: ______

Compounds: ______ 2 marks

(c) Give the symbol and chemical formula for each substance.

______ 3 marks

TOTAL

How did you score?

9 or less – try again!
10 – 15 – nearly there!
16 – 21 – well done!

ROCKS AND WEATHERING

Week 4 Thursday

What you need to know

1. Know about the processes of **weathering**, **erosion**, transportation and sedimentation.
2. Know that **evaporation** and dissolving are involved in the formation of some rocks.
3. Know that some processes take very long periods of time, while others can take a relatively short time.

WEATHERING

- All types of rock can be worn away, or eroded, by **weathering**.
- Weathering involves mechanical, chemical and organic processes.
- Different rock types are susceptible to different kinds of weathering.

Mechanical

- freeze–thaw;
- extreme temperature changes;
- bombardment by rocks and particles carried in the wind or in water.

Chemical

- dissolving by rainwater or groundwater;
- attack by acids in rainwater;
- oxidation with the atmosphere.

Organic

- plant roots push rocks apart;
- some plants absorb chemicals from rock;
- some molluscs use their shells to grind into rock.

In cold weather

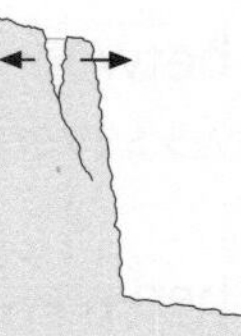

water collects in a crack, freezes and expands

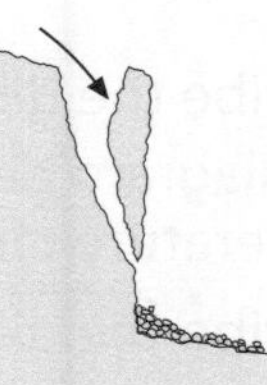

after time

In deserts

rock surface expands as it is heated and contracts as it cools

the rock surface breaks up

TRANSPORTATION

- Particles and substances from rocks are transported by wind and water away from the rock they came from.
- Fast flowing streams and rivers can move larger rocks but as the water slows, less can be carried.
- Strong winds can carry larger particles of dust, and as the wind gets slower, so the dust falls to the ground.

SEDIMENTATION

- As the water travels slower, and possibly evaporates, so the particles that were being carried settle out. As layer upon layer of particles settle, so new rock can begin to form. This can take an extremely long period of time.

ROCKS AND WEATHERING

1 The diagram below shows several stages in the process of freeze-thaw weathering.

A

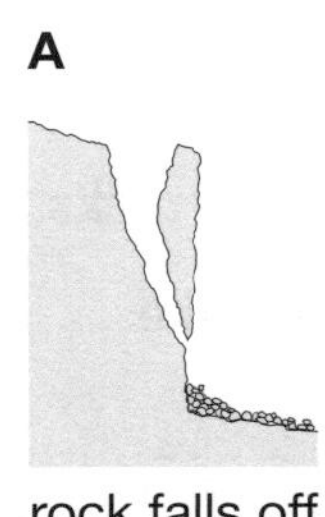

rock falls off

B

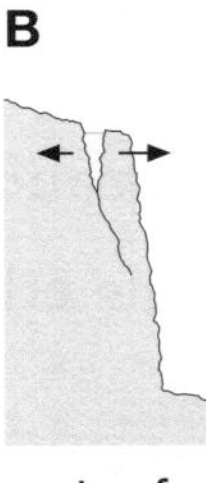

water freezes and expands

C

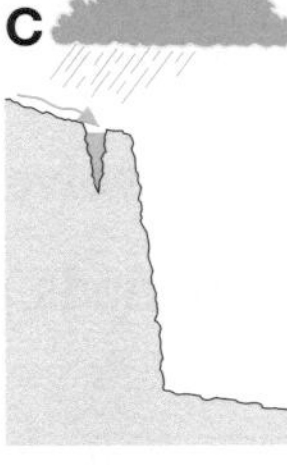

gap in the rock fills with water

What is the correct order for these stages?

______________________________ 2 marks

2 The diagram below shows several stages in the process of weathering due to temperature change.

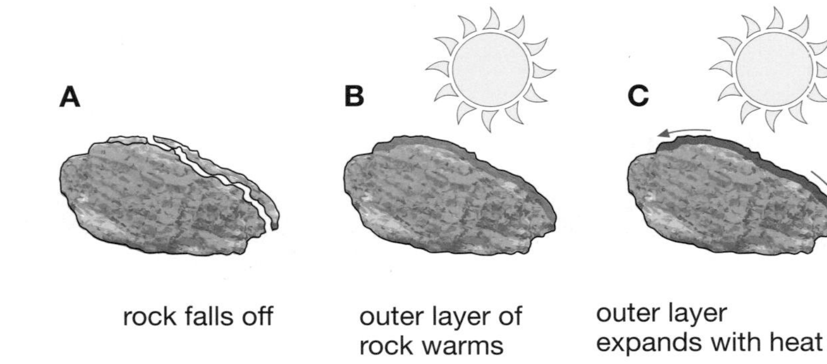

What is the correct order for these stages?

______________________________ 2 marks

3 Cliff faces at the seashore are eroded by the sea.
Explain **one** way in which the sea erodes the rocks.

______________________________ 2 marks

4 What is the name given to the process of carrying small particles of rock by wind or water?

______________________________ 1 mark

5 What is the name given to the process by which small particles of rock settle into layers?

______________________________ 1 mark

6 Large pieces of rock can be split by heating them and by pouring water along a line.
Explain how this technique splits the rock.

____

______________________________ 2 marks

TOTAL

How did you score?
4 or less – try again!
5 – 7 – nearly there!
8 – 10 – well done!

THE ROCK CYCLE

Week 4
Friday

What you need to know

1. Know the major rock-forming processes.
2. Know how to use the concept of rock texture as one of the key characteristics of **igneous**, **sedimentary** and **metamorphic rocks**.
3. Know how rock-forming processes are linked by the rock cycle.
4. Know how to relate processes such as crystallisation to processes involved in the rock cycle.
5. Know that some processes take very long periods of time, while others can take a very short time.

ROCK TYPES

- Most rocks are a mixture of crystals and grains of minerals. There are three main types:

Type of rock	Igneous	Sedimentary	Metamorphic
How it was made	Made when molten rock solidified.	Made as material was laid on top of other material. Weight forced the particles together to make rock.	Rock that has been changed by intense pressure and high temperature.
Features	The more slowly the rock solidified, the larger the crystals in the rock.	It is possible to see remnants of small creatures in some sedimentary rocks.	
Examples	pumice granite obsidian basalt	chalk limestone shale sandstone	slate marble quartzite

- Around the world, new rocks are constantly forming and old rocks are being worn away. This process is called the rock cycle.
- Some of the processes within the cycle can take extremely long periods of time, while others take a much shorter time.

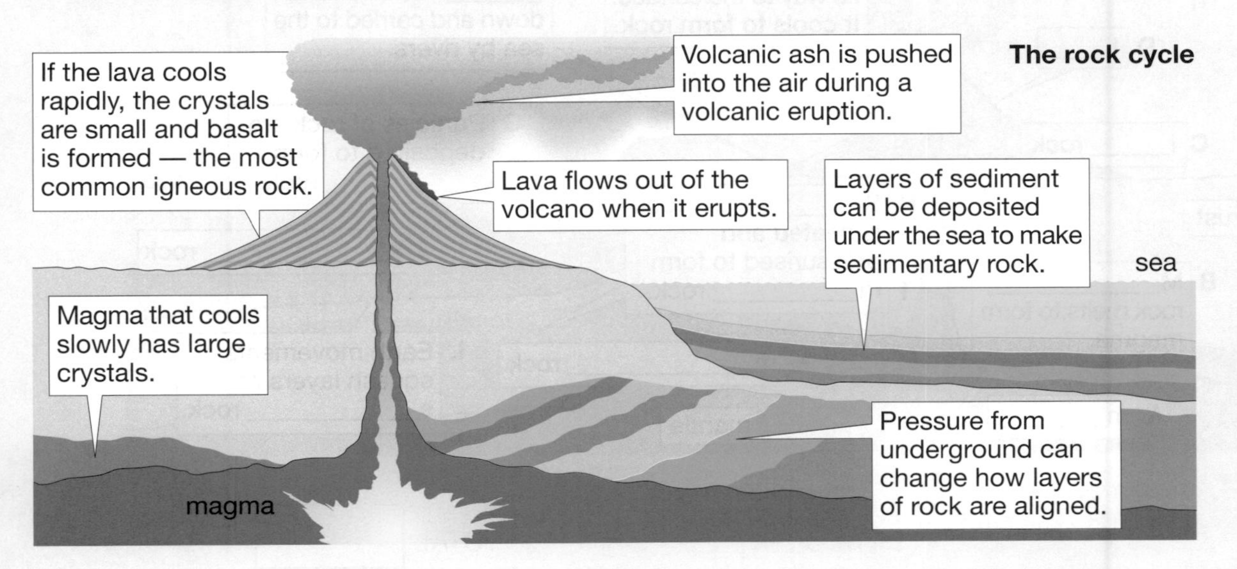

THE ROCK CYCLE

1 (a) You find a piece of rock that is white and has remnants of small creatures in it. Is it sedimentary, igneous or metamorphic rock?

______________________________ 1 mark

(b) Give a reason for your answer to part (a).

______________________________ 1 mark

2 Limestone is transformed into marble by intense heat and high pressure. What kind of rock is marble?

______________________________ 1 mark

3 Slate is a metamorphic rock, formed from shale.

(a) Describe **one** use of slate.

______________________________ 1 mark

(b) Explain why it is especially useful for this purpose.

______________________________ 1 mark

4 Marble is a metamorphic rock made from limestone.

(a) Describe **one** use of marble.

______________________________ 1 mark

(b) Describe **one** use of limestone.

______________________________ 1 mark

5 Explain the difference between **magma** and **lava**.

______________________________ 1 mark

6 The diagram below shows the rock cycle. Provide the missing labels for the diagram.

12 marks

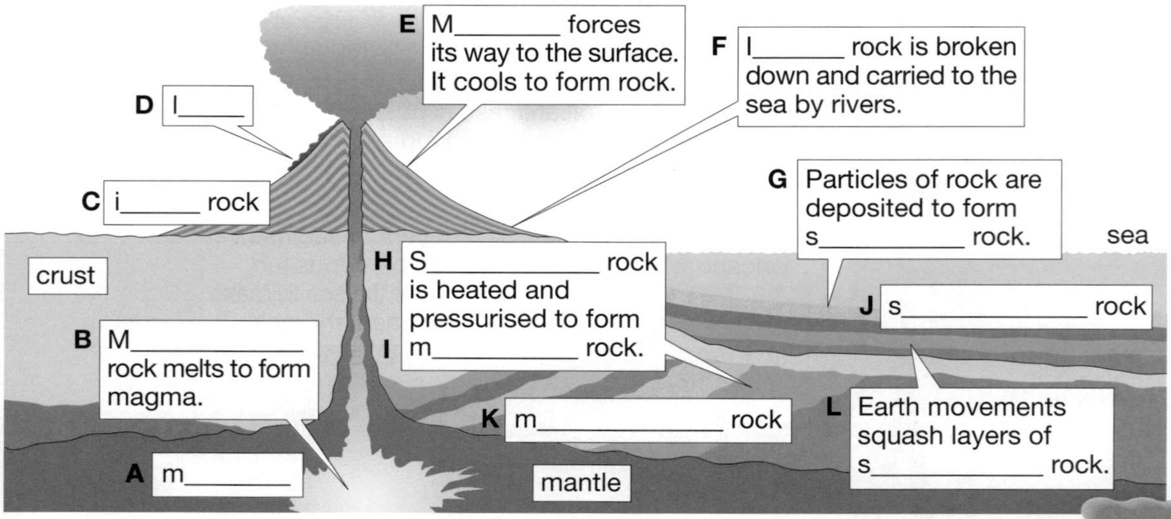

E M________ forces its way to the surface. It cools to form rock.
F I_______ rock is broken down and carried to the sea by rivers.
D I_____
C i_______ rock
G Particles of rock are deposited to form s___________ rock.
sea
crust
H S_____________ rock is heated and pressurised to form
I m____________ rock.
J s______________ rock
B M______________ rock melts to form magma.
K m_____________ rock
L Earth movements squash layers of s____________ rock.
A m________
mantle

TOTAL

How did you score?
9 or less – try again!
10 – 14 – nearly there!
15 – 20 – well done!

HEATING AND COOLING

Week 5
Monday

What you need to know

1. Know how to use a temperature scale to compare temperatures.
2. Know the difference between heat and temperature.
3. Know how heat is transferred by **conduction**, **convection** and **radiation.**
4. Know how to apply conduction, convection and radiation in familiar contexts.
5. Know how to use the particle model to explain expansion, conduction, convection and **change of state**.

MEASURING TEMPERATURE

- Temperature is measured in degrees Celsius (Note: NOT degrees centigrade).
- The boiling point of pure water at sea level is 100°C.
- The freezing point of pure water at sea level is 0°C.

WHAT IS HEAT?

- Heat is a form of energy. It is measured in joules.
- Particles with more heat energy move faster than those with less heat energy.
- A large object with a low temperature can have more heat energy than a small object with a high temperature.
- Heat energy can be transferred by **conduction**, **convection** and **radiation.**

Method of transfer	Conduction	Convection	Radiation
It works in	Metals	Liquids and gases (fluids)	Radiation can pass through a vacuum, air and transparent materials.
How it works	Vibrations are passed on from one atom to the next. Long regular arrangements of atoms can usually transfer heat well.	Warm fluids become low in density because of the spacing of the particles. Low density fluids rise and are replaced by higher density, cooler fluids. *Forced* convection involves blowing air over a hot element, so that the air is heated by conduction.	Electromagnetic radiation is emitted from all objects that contain heat energy. Humans cannot see this type of radiation. Non-shiny surfaces emit radiation sufficiently. Large areas emit more radiation than small areas.
How to stop it	Introduce a break in the solid, and place a material that does not conduct heat well into the gap.	Trap the fluid so it cannot move. Materials that trap pockets of air are effective insulators.	Use small surfaces that are highly polished or reflective. These emit radiation least.

EXPANSION

- When a particle in a solid gains heat energy, it vibrates faster. As a result, it pushes other particles away harder than before. With millions of particles all doing the same thing, the material expands and becomes larger.

CHANGE OF STATE

- If you keep heating a material, eventually the vibrations between atoms become so large that the bonds between the particles break and the atoms can move freely. This happens when a material melts. If you add even more heat energy it evaporates.

HEATING AND COOLING

1 A kettle that is shiny on the outside is less wasteful than one that is not shiny. Explain why.

1 mark

2 To lift a hot metal tray from an oven, a cook holds the tray with an oven glove.

(a) What kind of heat transfer does the glove prevent?

1 mark

(b) Explain why the glove acts in this way.

2 marks

3 Bill buys a cup of tea at a café. It is served in a polystyrene cup, with a plastic lid. Explain how both of these help to keep the tea from losing heat energy.

2 marks

4 The diagram below shows a device that can be fixed to a transistor to keep it cool. It is called a 'heat sink'.

(a) Explain why the heat sink has been shaped this way.

2 marks

(b) What is the advantage of painting the heat sink matt black?

1 mark

5 A microprocessor chip gets very hot even when operating normally. To help it to lose heat, it has a heat sink and a fan.

Explain how both of these devices work together to reduce the temperature of the chip.

3 marks

6 A tray in an oven is easy to slide in and out when the oven is cool, but becomes hard to move when the oven is hot. Explain this change.

2 marks

7 When it is cold, many people wear clothes that contain plenty of air, such as a woolly jumper. Explain why this type of clothing keeps you warm.

2 marks

TOTAL

How did you score?

7 or less – try again!
8 – 12 – nearly there!
13 – 16 – well done!

MAGNETS AND ELECTROMAGNETS

Week 5 Tuesday

What you need to know

1. Know what a **magnetic field** is.
2. Know the difference between a permanent magnet and an **electromagnet**.
3. Know the factors that affect the strength of an electromagnet.
4. Know how to identify magnetic materials, make a magnet and test the strength of a magnet.

WHAT IS A MAGNETIC FIELD?

- A **magnetic field** is an area where magnetism can be detected. It can be detected with special sensors, with a compass or with iron filings.
- Field lines can be used to represent the field by showing its 'shape'. The closer the field lines, the stronger the field.
- The north-seeking pole of the compass points in the direction of the magnetic field.

PERMANENT MAGNETS

- Certain materials like steel can become permanently magnetised. They have a 'north' and 'south' pole.
- If the magnet is suspended freely, the 'north pole' of the magnet faces towards the North. It is a 'north-seeking' pole.
- Like poles repel and opposite poles attract.
- The strength of a permanent magnet may be reduced by:
  - heat;
  - vibration.
- Other materials such as iron can be temporarily magnetised.

A bar magnet produces a magnetic field.

N S

ELECTROMAGNETS

- A wire carrying an electric current produces a magnetic field.
- The strength of the field can be increased by:
  - increasing the current;
  - winding the wire into a tight coil (a solenoid) with many turns;
  - using a magnetic material such as iron at the centre of the coil. This is called a 'core'.

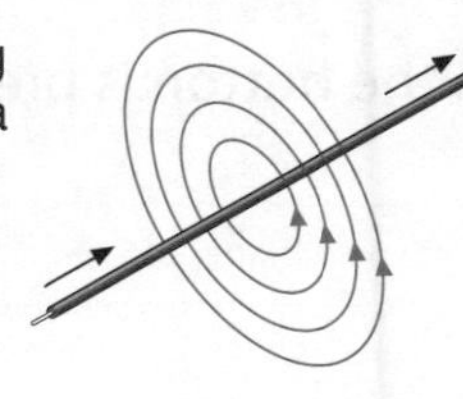
A wire carrying a current has a magnetic field around it.

A coil of wire carrying a current produces a magnetic field.

MAGNETS AND ELECTROMAGNETS

1 Iron can be used to make a permanent magnet. True or false?

1 mark

2 What is the name given to a coil of wire that is used to make a magnetic field?

1 mark

3 What is the name given to the material that is placed in the centre of the coil in an electromagnet?

1 mark

4 Write down **two** ways of reducing the strength of a permanent magnet.

2 marks

5 Write down **two** ways of increasing the strength of an electromagnet.

2 marks

6 Complete the diagrams below by showing the magnetic field around each magnet.

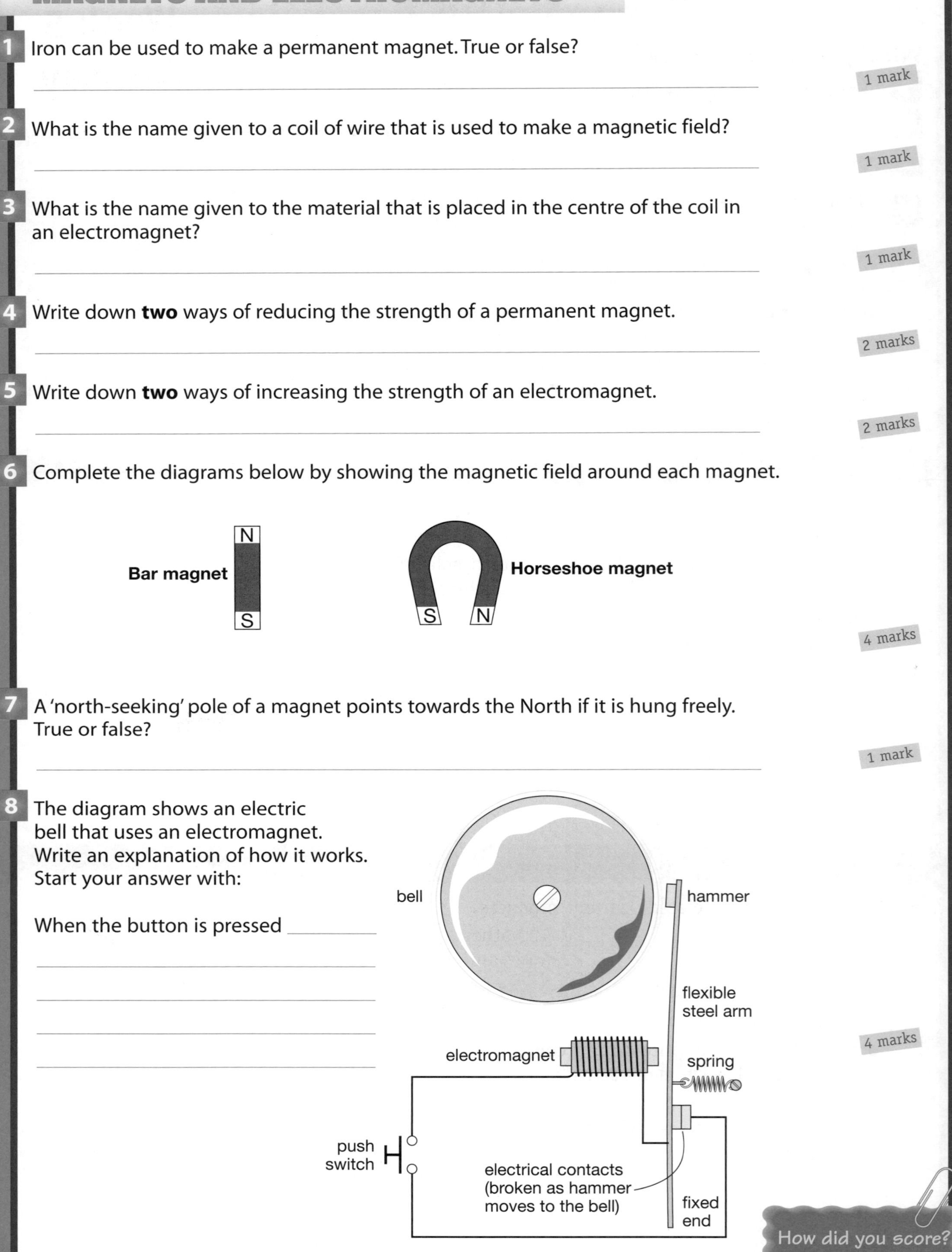

4 marks

7 A 'north-seeking' pole of a magnet points towards the North if it is hung freely. True or false?

1 mark

8 The diagram shows an electric bell that uses an electromagnet. Write an explanation of how it works. Start your answer with:

When the button is pressed ____________

4 marks

TOTAL

How did you score?

7 or less – try again!
8 – 12 – nearly there!
13 – 16 – well done!

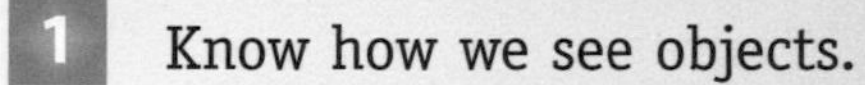

LIGHT

Week 5 Wednesday

What you need to know

1. Know how we see objects.
2. Know how to represent light as a ray and use this to explain reflection and **refraction**.
3. Know the difference between coloured light and white light.
4. Know why some objects are coloured.

HOW DO WE SEE?

- To see an object, our eyes detect light coming from it. The light might be radiated by a luminous object (such as a light bulb), or it may bounce off the object (such as the light from this book).
- Once the light reaches your eye, it is focused onto nerves at the back of your eye and a signal is sent to your brain.

HOW DOES LIGHT TRAVEL?

- Light normally travels at very high speed in a straight line. The direction of the light may be changed if it is reflected or refracted.
- Any shiny surface can reflect light.
- Anything that is transparent, such as water or glass, can refract light.
- **Transparent** materials transmit the light and allow the light to pass straight through.
- **Translucent** materials allow light to pass, but change the direction of travel in a random way so you cannot see a clear image through them.
- Materials that absorb light are called **opaque**.

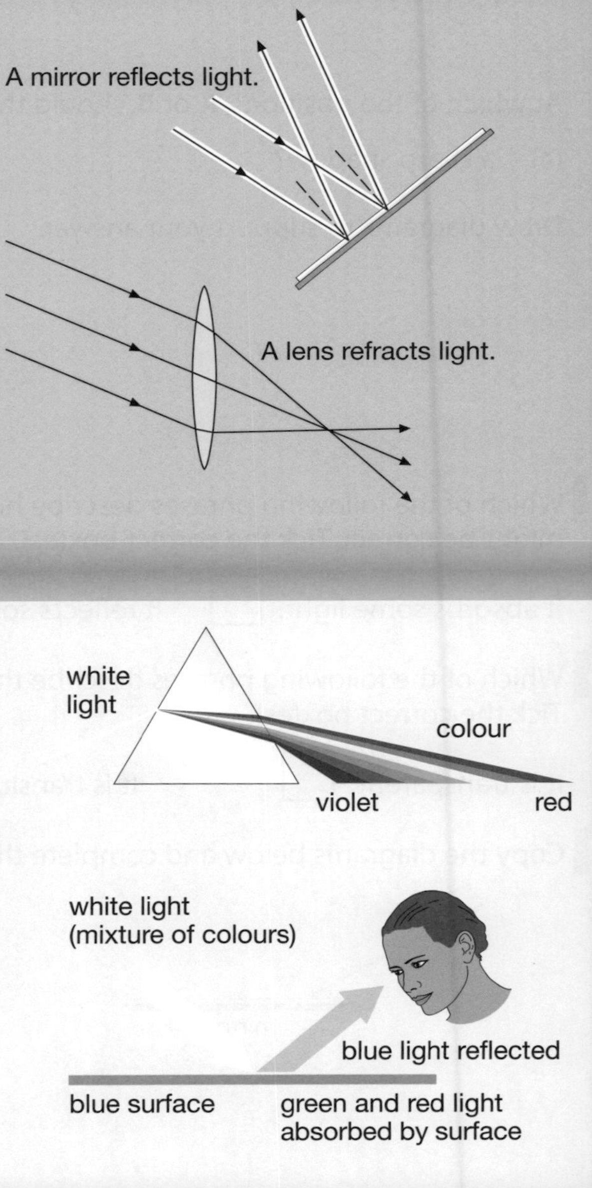

IS LIGHT COLOURED?

- All light rays are coloured, but if there is a wide range of colours all mixed in together, the light looks white.
- If white light passes through a prism, the different colours of light can be separated out.
- When white light (i.e. light containing all colours) hits an object, some colours are absorbed by the object, and the other colours are reflected. The object appears coloured because it only reflects some colours of light to your eye.

1 Describe how you would recognise a 'translucent material'.

1 mark

2 Describe how you would recognise a 'transparent' material.

1 mark

3 To make a shadow, some light must be blocked by a material, while other light passes around the object.
What properties must the material have to cast a shadow? Tick the correct box(es).

It must be transparent. ☐ It must be translucent. ☐ It must be opaque. ☐

1 mark

4 The diagram below shows how a shadow can be cast by an object.

shadow
torch
A
B
screen

At which of the positions, **A** or **B**, should the object be placed to produce:

(a) a sharp shadow? ______ (b) a large shadow? ______

Draw diagrams to support your answer.

2 marks

5 Which of the following phrases describe how this page affects light. More than one might be correct. Tick the correct box(es).

It absorbs some light. ☐ It reflects some light. ☐ It radiates some light. ☐

2 marks

6 Which of the following phrases describe this page? More than one might be correct. Tick the correct box(es).

It is transparent. ☐ It is translucent. ☐ It is opaque. ☐

1 mark

7 Copy the diagrams below and complete them to show the path that the light will follow.

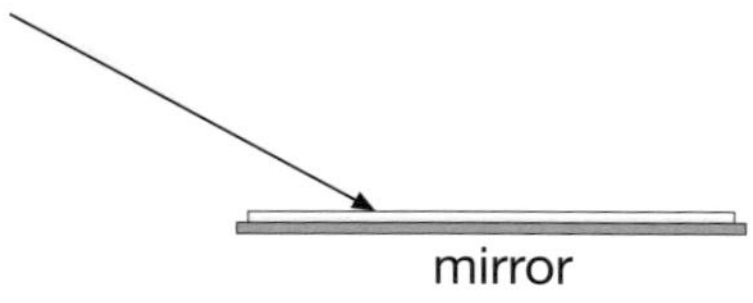

mirror

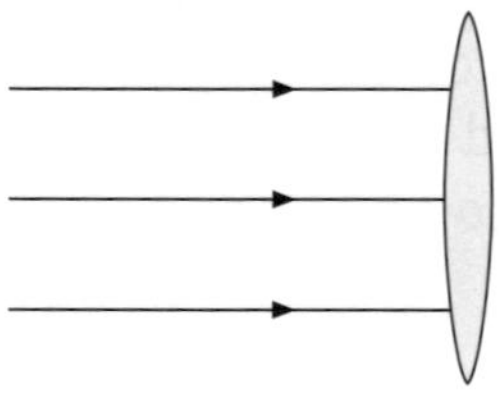

4 marks

TOTAL ☐

How did you score?
5 or less – try again!
6 – 8 – nearly there!
9 – 12 – well done!

SOUND AND HEARING

What you need to know

1. Know how sound is produced.
2. Know how sound travels through solids, liquids and gases.
3. Know how to compare sounds.
4. Know how the ear works.
5. Know that loud noise can be harmful and how loud noise can be reduced.

HOW IS SOUND MADE?

- Sound is made by an object that is vibrating or oscillating quickly.
- To produce a sound, the object must oscillate between 20 and 20 000 times a second.
- The vibrating object passes the vibration to particles in the air, or another medium, and they in turn pass the vibration on. In this way, sound spreads as a compression wave.
- Sound needs a substance to carry it. It cannot pass through a vacuum.

HOW DO WE DESCRIBE SOUNDS?

- We hear low frequency oscillations as sound with a low pitch (the bass notes). High frequency oscillations produce sounds with a high pitch (the treble notes).
- Strong oscillations have a large amplitude and produce a loud sound. Weak oscillations have a small amplitude and produce a quiet sound.
- Normal sounds vary in loudness. This variation is called the dynamics of the sound.

EXPERIMENTING WITH SOUNDS

- A microphone attached to an oscilloscope can show the pattern of the sound being detected.

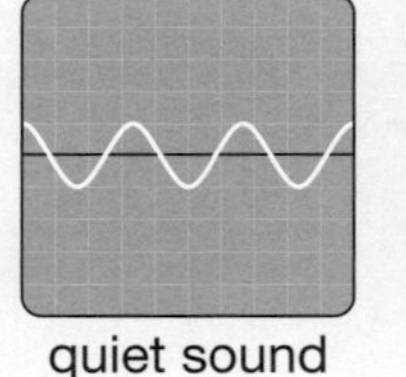
quiet sound

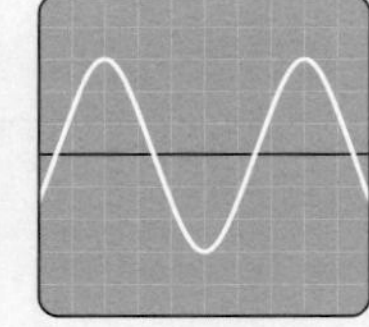
loud sound

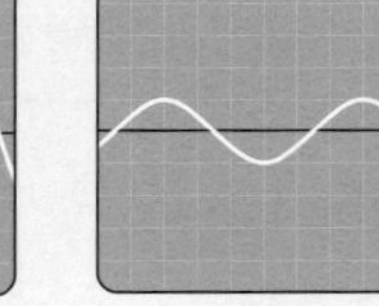
low frequency sound

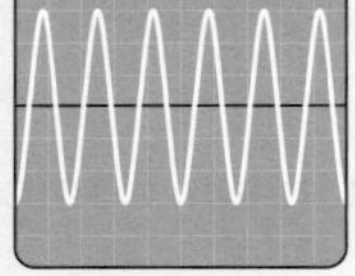
high frequency sound

- A tuning fork produces a very pure sound with just one frequency.
- A signal generator and a loudspeaker can produce a range of frequencies and types of sound.

HOW WE HEAR SOUND

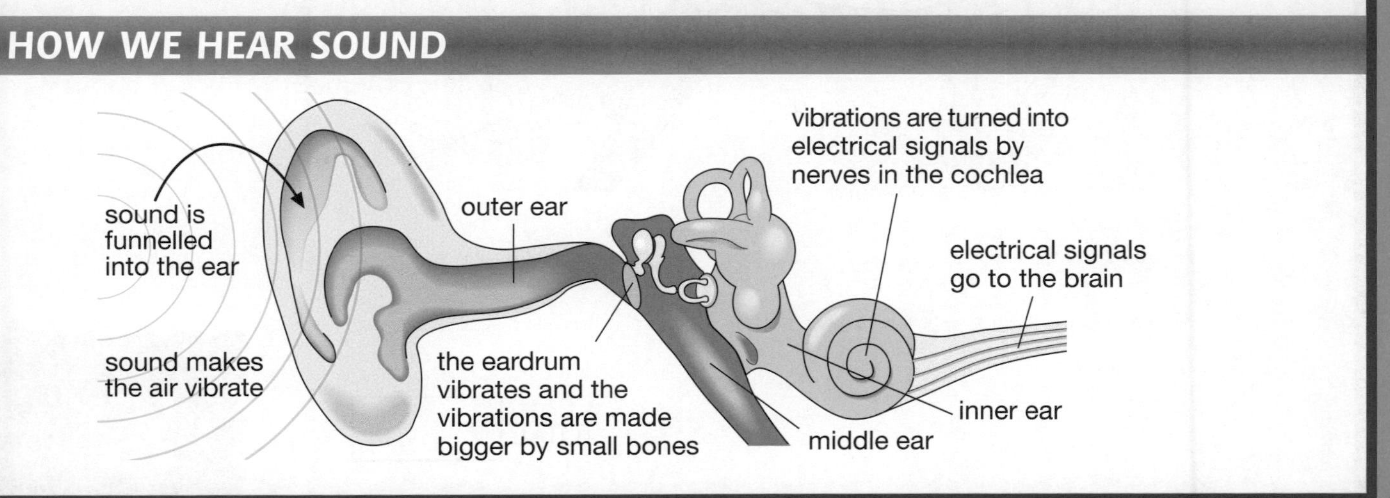

SOUND AND HEARING

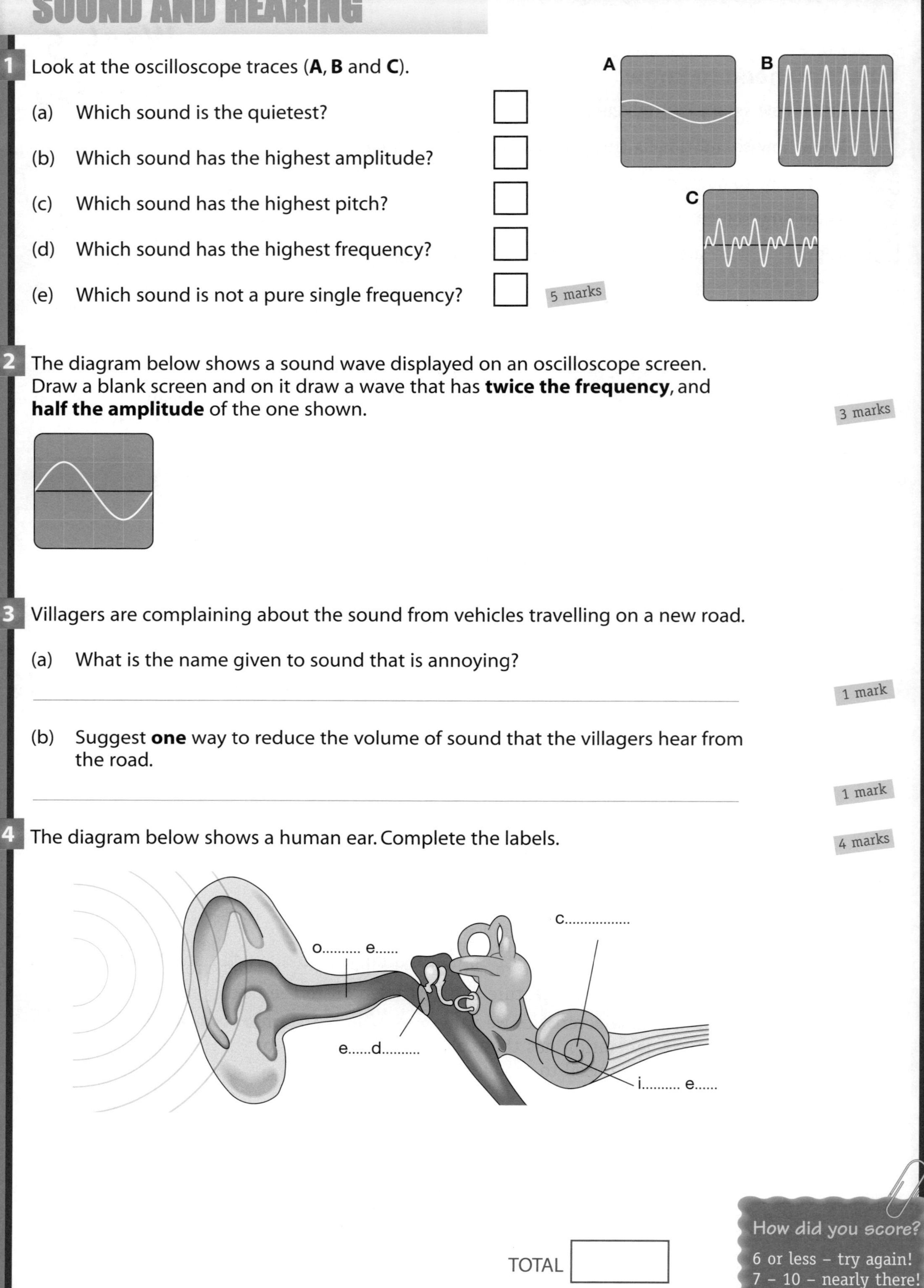

1 Look at the oscilloscope traces (**A**, **B** and **C**).

A B C

(a) Which sound is the quietest? ☐

(b) Which sound has the highest amplitude? ☐

(c) Which sound has the highest pitch? ☐

(d) Which sound has the highest frequency? ☐

(e) Which sound is not a pure single frequency? ☐

5 marks

2 The diagram below shows a sound wave displayed on an oscilloscope screen. Draw a blank screen and on it draw a wave that has **twice the frequency**, and **half the amplitude** of the one shown.

3 marks

3 Villagers are complaining about the sound from vehicles travelling on a new road.

(a) What is the name given to sound that is annoying?

____

1 mark

(b) Suggest **one** way to reduce the volume of sound that the villagers hear from the road.

____

1 mark

4 The diagram below shows a human ear. Complete the labels.

4 marks

o.......... e......

c.................

e......d..........

i.......... e......

TOTAL ☐

How did you score?

6 or less – try again!
7 – 10 – nearly there!
11 – 14 – well done!

INHERITANCE AND SELECTION

Week 5
Friday

What you need to know

1. Know that characteristics are inherited.
2. Know about variations arising from environmental differences.
3. Know how knowledge of inherited characteristics is used in selective breeding.
4. Know why selective breeding is important.

HUMAN LIFE CYCLE

- The human life cycle includes the stages: baby - toddler - child - adolescent - adult.
- Once an individual has grown into an adult, they are capable of reproduction.
- When born, a baby needs nurturing and protection. This period normally lasts until they are an independent adult.
- This period of time is much longer in humans than in other animals.

INHERITANCE

- Many of our features are determined by the genes we inherit from our parents. These features include:
  - hair, eye and skin colour;
  - facial proportions (the shape of our face);
  - proportions of our body (the shape of our body);
  - blood type.
- In addition, there are skills and abilities that we can inherit. These may include:
  - strength;
  - ability to run long distances.
- The environment is also important. We may have the genes to grow tall, but this will only happen if we also have a healthy diet.
- There is also random variation. Genes are not always copied accurately from one generation to the next and genes are mixed from both parents to give the offspring.

SELECTIVE BREEDING

- In any group of animals or plants, there is variation. Some plants may be taller than others and some animals may be able to run faster than others in their group. If this feature is due to their genes, the feature can be passed on to the next generation.
- Animals or plants with characteristics we value can be bred together to increase the chance that the next generation has these characteristics. The process of choosing which organisms should be used to produce the next generation is called selective breeding.

INHERITANCE AND SELECTION

1 Give the general name of features that we inherit from our parents.

______________________________ 1 mark

2 Bill and Mary are both fast runners.

(a) Explain why their baby is quite likely to grow to be a fast runner too.

______________________________ 1 mark

(b) Give **two** reasons why their baby might not grow to be a fast runner.

______________________________ 2 marks

3 In selective breeding, it is important to have variation in the population you want to breed from. Explain why variation is important for successful selective breeding.

______________________________ 2 marks

4 Below is a list of human characteristics. Decide whether each one is due to genes only, due to environment only or due to a mixture of genes and environment.

natural hair colour ______________ actual hair colour ______________

skin colour ______________ eye colour ______________

weight ______________ height ______________

footballing skills ______________ hair length ______________ 8 marks

5 Almost all the food we eat comes from plants or animals that have been selectively bred over many years to improve their quality or to improve another important feature.

Join the plant or animal to the valued feature.

Plant or animal		**Selectively bred to...**	
A	cow	1	grow short trees so they are easier to pick
B	pig	2	be less aggressive
C	mandarin orange	3	have larger and more abundant seeds
D	wheat	4	produce meat with little fat
E	apple	5	produce more milk
F	bull	6	have no seeds

6 marks

TOTAL [ ]

How did you score?
9 or less – try again!
10 – 14 – nearly there!
15 – 20 – well done!

What you need to know

1. Know how the human respiratory, digestive and circulatory systems interact to keep us alive.
2. Know about the functions of the skeleton.
3. Know about ways in which diet, exercise, smoking and drugs affect health.

IMPORTANT SYSTEMS

- The cells in your body need food and **oxygen** and must get rid of waste products. Three systems work together to do this task.

The circulatory system

- It includes heart, **veins** and **arteries**.
- The heart pumps blood to your body through arteries. It comes back through veins.
- The muscles in your heart are strengthened by moderate exercise.

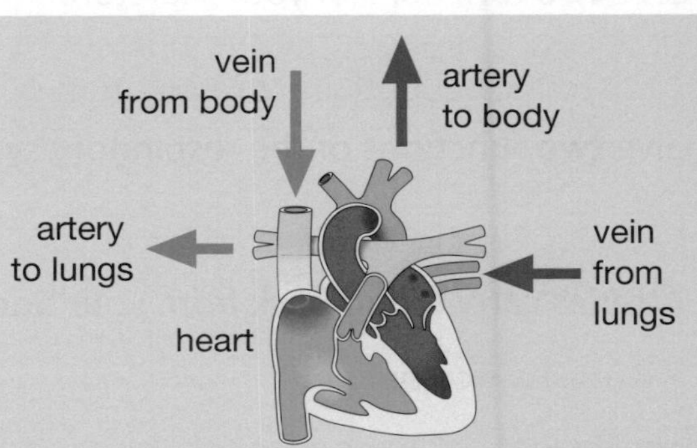

A heart has two pumps linked together.

The respiratory system

- It takes oxygen into your body.
- It gets rid of carbon dioxide from your body.
- Blood carries these gases between the cells and the lungs.
- Avoiding smoking keeps the lungs clean so they can work effectively.

The digestive system

- It breaks food into small molecules that your body can absorb.
- It gets rid of waste materials.
- Blood carries the molecules between your gut and your cells.
- A healthy diet includes a variety of foods.
- Eating roughage helps the muscles in your gut to push food along.

These systems are kept in delicate balance by messages to your brain.

- Drugs can artificially stimulate your body systems, and can also block important messages from reaching your brain. This can cause permanent damage and even death.
- Smoking is dangerous as tobacco smoke contains nicotine, which is very addictive, and many other poisonous chemicals. Alcohol can also damage your body.

BONES IN YOUR BODY

- Your skeleton:
  - protects vital organs (e.g. the skull protects the brain, the ribs protect the heart and lungs);
  - gives you mobility, allowing you to move about.
- Large bones also make blood.
- To keep your bones healthy, ensure that your diet contains enough calcium.
- Regular exercise keeps your bones strong.

FIT AND HEALTHY

1 Which **two** systems start to work harder when you exercise?

_______________ 2 marks

2 Which system is particularly damaged by smoking?

_______________ 1 mark

3 Which system is particularly damaged by eating 'junk food', which contains no roughage.

_______________ 1 mark

4 Give **two** functions of your skeleton.

_______________ 2 marks

5 Give **two** functions of the respiratory system.

_______________ 2 marks

6 'Arteries carry blood back from your body to your heart.' True or false?

_______________ 1 mark

7 What is the name of the substance in tobacco smoke that makes smoking addictive?

_______________ 1 mark

8 A person who stops breathing will die. Explain why.

_______________ 1 mark

9 A person whose heart stops beating will die. Explain why.

_______________ 1 mark

10 The diagram below shows an alveolus which is part of your lung.
Label the gases and the other part that is indicated.

3 marks

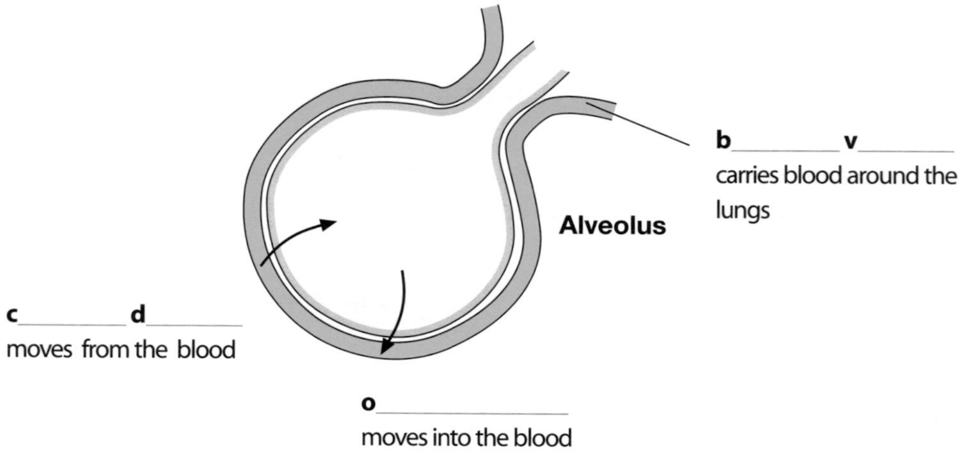

TOTAL

How did you score?
6 or less – try again!
7 – 11 – nearly there!
12 – 15 – well done!

PLANTS AND PHOTOSYNTHESIS

Week 6
Tuesday

What you need to know

1. Know that **photosynthesis** is the key process that enables plants to grow.
2. Know the importance of photosynthesis to humans and other animals.
3. Know how to describe photosynthesis using a word equation.
4. Know that the carbon dioxide for photosynthesis comes from the air and that the water is absorbed through the roots.
5. Know that **chlorophyll** enables a plant to utilise light in photosynthesis.
6. Know the role of the leaf in photosynthesis.

WHAT IS PHOTOSYNTHESIS?

- **Photosynthesis** enables plants to grow.
- Because all food webs start with plants, photosynthesis is essential for all life on Earth.
- Photosynthesis may be described by the following word equation:

carbon dioxide (from the air) + water (absorbed through roots) → oxygen + starch

- The reaction needs light energy to work. This energy is collected by **chlorophyll**, a chemical found in some plant cells. Chlorophyll is green.
- Many leaves are thin and flat and therefore have a large surface area. This allows them to absorb large amounts of sunlight, as well as allowing easy movement of gases into and out of the leaf.
- To enable photosynthesis to happen, other chemicals are needed. This is called plant food, or fertiliser. These chemicals must be absorbed by the roots, or they can even be obtained by the plant capturing insects and digesting them!

SPECIAL PLANTS

- Conifers are adapted to living in cold climates and have leaves shaped like needles. A flat leaf would be damaged by heavy falls of snow, but snow can fall easily through the fine needle-shaped leaves.
- Mosses and ferns are some of the oldest plants on Earth. They usually have small root systems compared to other plants, such as trees. As a result they survive best in damp conditions, where water is easily available.

PLANTS AND PHOTOSYNTHESIS

1 Complete the following word equation for photosynthesis.

carbon dioxide + water → ______________________ + starch

1 mark

2 Give the names of **two** gases that are involved in photosynthesis.

____

2 marks

3 A small tree was planted in a pot of soil. It was watered regularly, but no fertiliser was added. After five years the tree was weighed and was found to have gained weight.

Where did most of the extra weight come from? Tick the correct box(es).

the water ☐ the soil ☐ the air ☐

1 mark

4 Plants are essential for animals to survive because of the **oxygen** and **starch** they produce and because of the **carbon dioxide** they remove from the air. Explain why each of these three aspects is important to animals.

____

3 marks

5 A tropical fish tank contains a number of small fish, several small plants and a light.

light

Tropical fish tank

air pump

(a) Explain why it is important that there is a light in the fish tank.

____

1 mark

(b) Describe what would happen to the fish if the light stopped working.

____

2 marks

TOTAL ☐

How did you score?

4 or less – try again!
5 – 7 – nearly there!
8 – 10 – well done!

PLANTS FOR FOOD

What you need to know

1. Know that humans are part of a complex food web.
2. Know about factors that affect plant growth.
3. Know how management of food production has many implications for other animal and plant populations in the environment.
4. Know some of the issues involved in sustainable development of the countryside.

A VARIED DIET

- Many humans eat a wide variety of foods.
- The diet of someone in the UK may consist of primary producers (e.g. rice, potatoes), primary consumers (e.g. chicken, sheep) and some carnivores (e.g. cod, tuna).
- In the UK, food is imported from around the world.
- This means that a food web involving humans in the UK is extremely complex.

A RESTRICTED DIET

- Some humans live on restricted diets. This can lead to health problems.
- Energy is lost from food chains at each stage. To support large numbers of people from a limited amount of land, short food chains are needed because they are more efficient.
- Farming just one food crop reduces the diversity of plants and animals in an area.
- A crop of only one kind of plant is called a monoculture.
- Longer food chains are needed to support humans where soil quality is poor.

Example lichen and poor quality grass → reindeer → Laplander
poor quality grass → cows → Maasai

FARMING STYLES

- To keep the price of food low, some farms in the UK use:
  - very large fields;
  - large machines to sow and reap crops;
  - large amounts of artificial fertiliser;
  - cheap labour from migrant workers;
  - subsidies from governments and the European Union.
- To improve farming efficiency some farmers remove hedges causing:
  - lack of nesting sites and cover for animals, thus lowering biodiversity;
  - increased risk of soil erosion.

PLANTS FOR FOOD

1 Give **two** primary producers eaten by humans.

2 marks

2 Give **two** primary consumers eaten by humans.

2 marks

3 Give **two** carnivores eaten by humans.

2 marks

4 Explain why short food chains are the best way of feeding very large numbers of people.

1 mark

5 Explain why many people must eat meat to survive in their environment.

1 mark

6 Some farmers remove hedges from their land.

(a) Explain why a farmer might do this.

2 marks

(b) Describe the impact this has on the environment.

2 marks

(c) Describe **one** impact of insisting that farmers do not use artificial fertilisers and that they keep their fields small.

1 mark

7 The foodweb below is for a farm.
Use it to answer the questions that follow.

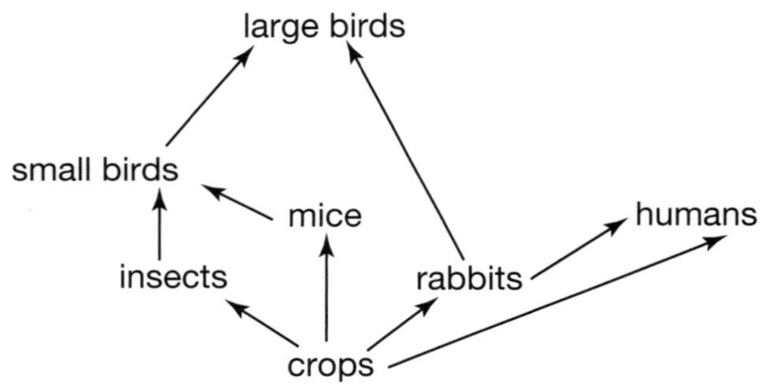

Describe the impact on the food web of the following events:

(a) Spraying the crop with an insecticide

1 mark

(b) Removing hedges

1 mark

(c) Shooting hawks

1 mark

TOTAL

How did you score?
7 or less – try again!
8 – 12 – nearly there!
13 – 16 – well done!

REACTIONS WITH METALS

Week 6 Thursday

What you need to know

1. Know the differences between **metals** and **non-metals.**
2. Know that different acids react in similar ways with metals, with metal carbonates and with metal oxides.
3. Know how to represent elements by symbols and compounds by formulae.
4. Know how to use word and symbol equations to describe these reactions.

METALS AND NON-METALS

- 89 out of the 109 known elements are **metals.**
- Metals are excellent conductors of electricity.
- Metals are excellent conductors of heat.
- Pure metals are shiny.
- Metals can be hit into shape (they are malleable).
- Metals can react to produce carbonates and oxides as well as many other compounds.
- Carbon is NOT a metal.

Examples of metals

Name	Symbol
Gold	Au
Silver	Ag
Copper	Cu
Iron	Fe
Sodium	Na
Lead	Pb
Potassium	K

Examples of metal carbonates

Compound name	Formula
Calcium carbonate (limestone)	$CaCO_3$
Magnesium carbonate	$MgCO_3$
Sodium carbonate	Na_2CO_3
Potassium carbonate	K_2CO_3

Examples of metal oxides

Compound name	Formula
Copper oxide	CuO
Lead oxide	PbO
Sodium oxide	Na_2O
Aluminium oxide	Al_2O_3
Iron oxide (rust)	Fe_2O_3

non-metals; metals; semiconductors

																	He
Li	Be											B	C	N	O	F	Ne
Na	Mg											Al	Si	P	S	Cl	Ar
K	Ca	Sc	Ti	V	Cr	Mn	Fe	Co	Ni	Cu	Zn	Ga	Ge	As	Se	Br	Kr
Rb	Sr	Y	Zr	Nb	Mo	Tc	Ru	Rh	Pd	Ag	Cd	In	Sn	Sb	Te	I	Xe
Cs	Ba	La	Hf	Ta	W	Re	Os	Ir	Pt	Au	Hg	Tl	Pb	Bi	Po	At	Rn
Fr	Ra	Ac															

METAL REACTIONS

- Metals and metal compounds react in similar ways with water and acids. More reactive metals react with water. Less reactive metals need acid to carry out the same sorts of reactions.

- metal + water → metal hydroxide + hydrogen
  e.g. sodium + water → sodium hydroxide + hydrogen
- metal oxide + water → metal hydroxide
  e.g. sodium oxide + water → sodium hydroxide
- metal + acid → metal salt + hydrogen
  e.g. zinc + sulphuric acid → zinc sulphate + hydrogen
- metal oxide + acid → metal salt + water
  e.g. copper oxide + sulphuric acid → copper sulphate + water
- metal carbonate + acid → metal salt + water + carbon dioxide
  e.g. calcium carbonate + acid → calcium chloride + water + carbon dioxide

REACTIONS WITH METALS

1 Give **two** characteristics of metals.

______________________________ 2 marks

2 Name **two** metals and write down their symbols.

______________________________ 2 marks

3 What is the chemical name for common rust? ______________________________ 1 mark

4 What is the chemical name of limestone and marble? ______________________________ 1 mark

5 When metals or metal oxides react with an acid, what substance is **always** produced?

______________________________ 1 mark

6 When hydrochloric acid is added to limestone a gas is released. What is the name of this gas?

______________________________ 1 mark

7 Complete these word equations:

(a) metal + water → ______________ + ______________ 2 marks

(b) metal oxide + water → ______________ 1 mark

(c) metal + acid → ______________ + ______________ 2 marks

(d) metal oxide + acid → ______________ + ______________ 2 marks

(e) metal carbonate + acid → ______________ + ______________ + ______________ 3 marks

8 Write a word equation for the following reaction:

$2CaCO_3 + 2HCl \rightarrow 2CaCl + H_2O + 2CO_2$

______________ + ______________ → ______________ + ______________ + ______________ 5 marks

9 Write a word equation for the following reaction:

$Na_2O + H_2O \rightarrow 2NaOH$

______________ + ______________ → ______________ 3 marks

10 Write a word equation for the following reaction:

$CuO + H_2SO_4 \rightarrow Cu\ SO_4 + H_2O$

______________ + ______________ → ______________ + ______________ 4 marks

TOTAL [ ]

How did you score?

13 or less – try again!
14 – 23 – nearly there!
24 – 30 – well done!

PATTERNS OF REACTIVITY

Week 6 Friday

What you need to know

1. Know that all metals react in a similar way with oxygen, water and acids, but some react more readily than others.
2. Know how to represent chemical reactions by word and/or symbol equations.
3. Know how to show and use the reactivity series for metals.

METALS AND REACTIVITY

- Metals react in similar ways with oxygen, acids and water. They produce similar kinds of products during the reactions:
  - metal + oxygen → metal oxide
  - metal + water → metal hydroxide + hydrogen
  - metal + acid → metal salt + hydrogen

REACTIVITY SERIES

- Some metals are highly reactive (potassium and sodium are very reactive with air and water).
- Some metals are unreactive (gold and platinum).
- The different reactivities of metals can be shown by carrying out reactions with air, water and acids and observing the rate at which they happen (e.g. by looking at the rate at which gas is released or the rate at which the metal loses its shine).
- Some reactions involving metals are extremely violent.

The reactivity series of some metals can be remembered using the following sentence:
'**P**lease **S**end **C**harles **M**onkeys **A**nd **Z**ebras **I**n **L**ead **C**ages' **S**he **G**asped **P**laintively.

P = potassium
S = sodium
C = calcium
M = magnesium
A = aluminium
Z = zinc
I = iron
L = lead
C = copper
S = silver
G = gold
P = platinum

more reactive

less reactive

USING THE REACTIVITY SERIES

- A more reactive metal will displace a less reactive metal from its ore. This kind of reaction is called a **displacement reaction**.
- The reactivity of a metal determines how the metal is extracted from its ore.
- Unreactive metals are found in the Earth's crust as elements.
- Low reactivity metals are extracted from their ores by heating them with carbon.
- Very reactive metals (e.g. aluminium) are extracted from their ore using electricity.
- In situations where tarnishing needs to be avoided, low reactivity metals are used.

Examples platinum, gold and silver jewellery;
gold for essential electrical contacts.

PATTERNS OF REACTIVITY

1 The Thermit reaction can be described by the following word equation:

iron oxide + aluminium → aluminium oxide + iron

(a) Explain why the reaction occurs. ______ 2 marks

(b) What is the name of this kind of reaction? ______ 1 mark

2 Artists in Middle Ages used thin gold to highlight religious figures in their paintings. Explain why gold was used instead of copper which was less expensive.

______ 1 mark

3 In the 1970s, gold was used for electrical contacts in some computers to ensure a good electrical contact.

(a) Explain why gold was the preferred metal for this function.

______ 1 mark

(b) Suggest why copper is used on modern computers instead of gold.

______ 1 mark

4 Old ships used iron nails to hold the planks of wood together. However, over time the nails corroded and the planks fell apart.
Explain why many shipbuilders preferred to use copper nails on the ships they built.

______ 1 mark

5 List the following metals in order of reactivity. Put the **most** reactive metal **first**.

calcium copper potassium platinum

______ 3 marks

6 List the following metals in order of reactivity. Put the **most** reactive metal **first**.

copper sodium gold aluminium zinc

______ 4 marks

7 The method of extraction depends on the reactivity of the metal.

(a) Join the metal to the method of extraction.

gold	using electricity
aluminium	heating it with carbon
iron	found as an element in rock

3 marks

(b) Based on the information above, suggest how silver is obtained from the Earth's crust.

______ 1 mark

8 Why are sodium and potassium stored by immersing them in oil, rather than just placing them in a jar in air?

______ 2 marks

TOTAL

How did you score?
9 or less – try again!
10 – 14 – nearly there!
15 – 20 – well done!

CHEMISTRY IN THE ENVIRONMENT

Week 7 Monday

What you need to know

1. Know that rocks, soils and building materials have a variety of chemical characteristics.
2. Know that chemical **weathering** alters rocks and building materials.
3. Know how the atmosphere and water resources are affected by natural processes and the activity of humans.
4. Know how environmental conditions are monitored and controlled.

ROCK EROSION

- Some rocks are more easily eroded than others. This can be because:
  - their particles are held together weakly (sandstone);
  - they dissolve more easily in rainwater than other rocks;
  - they react with acids in rainwater and groundwater more than other rocks (e.g. limestone reacts very well).
- These processes affect buildings as well as rock formations because many buildings are made from rock (e.g. sandstone, ironstone, granite, marble).

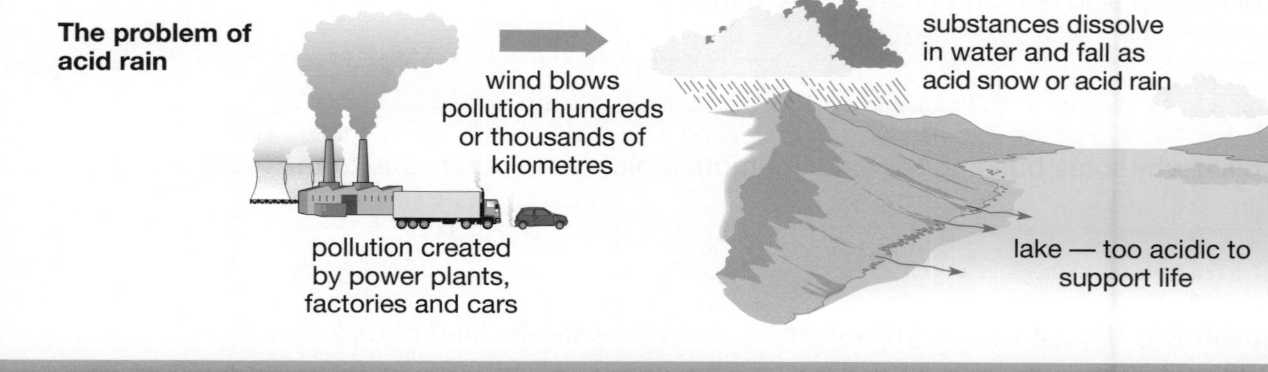

SOILS

- In many places, the characteristics of the soil depend on the rock underneath the soil.
- The rocks affect the acidity of the soil on top of it.
- Many plants are adapted to growing in soil with a particular acidity.

IMPACT OF HUMANS

- Burning fossil fuels in power stations and cars, puts acidic gases into the atmosphere.
- The gases dissolve in water and fall to earth as acid rain or acid snow.
- Acid rain damages trees and other plants.
- In spring, the snow melts, suddenly releasing large amounts of acidic water into streams and lakes.
- The rapid change in acidity kills many fish, and in turn the animals that rely on the fish as a food source. Acid lake water also helps poisonous chemicals like aluminium to dissolve and so get into living things.

CONTROLLING ENVIRONMENTAL CONDITIONS

- Crushed limestone can be added to polluted lakes to neutralise the acidity.

CHEMISTRY IN THE ENVIRONMENT

1 Describe **two** causes of acid rain.

2 marks

2 Explain what is meant by the term **groundwater**.

1 mark

3 Describe **one** way to reduce the acidity of a lake.

1 mark

4 Explain why the pH of some streams and lakes changes rapidly in springtime.

2 marks

5 The number of birds of prey has reduced in areas where there is acid rain.

Explain how acid rain may cause this to happen.

2 marks

6 Explain why some buildings deteriorate more rapidly than others due to the weather.

2 marks

7 Explain why the plants that grow in an area can indicate the kind of rock that is under the area.

2 marks

TOTAL

How did you score?

5 or less – try again!
6 – 8 – nearly there!
9 – 12 – well done!

USING CHEMISTRY

Week 7
Tuesday

What you need to know

1. Know that a **chemical reaction** involves a rearrangement of atoms.
2. Know that matter is not lost during a chemical reaction.
3. Know how chemical reactions are used to make new materials.
4. Know how chemical reactions can be used as a source of **energy**.
5. Know how to represent chemical reactions by word and/or symbol equations.

WHAT IS A CHEMICAL REACTION?

- Any **chemical reaction** involves a rearrangement of atoms.
- In a reaction, bonds between atoms break, and new ones form with different atoms.
- No atoms are 'lost' in a reaction. All atoms present in reactants are present in the products.
- The products can have very different properties from the reactants.

EXOTHERMIC AND ENDOTHERMIC REACTIONS

- Exothermic reactions release **energy** which we detect as heat or light.
- Burning any fuel involves an exothermic reaction.
- Endothermic reactions require energy to make them happen.
- Photosynthesis is an endothermic reaction – the energy is supplied by light.

Reactions to remember

- Cooking with natural gas involves burning methane in oxygen:
  methane + oxygen → carbon dioxide + water
  $CH_4 + 2O_2 \rightarrow CO_2 + 2H_2O$
- Photosynthesis involves combining carbon dioxide with water to make glucose. This is an endothermic reaction:
  carbon dioxide + water → glucose + oxygen
  $6CO_2 + 6H_2O \rightarrow C_6H_{12}O_6 + 6O_2$
- Respiration involves reacting glucose with oxygen. This is an exothermic reaction:
  glucose + oxygen → carbon dioxide + water
  $C_6H_{12}O_6 + 6O_2 \rightarrow 6CO_2 + 6H_2O$

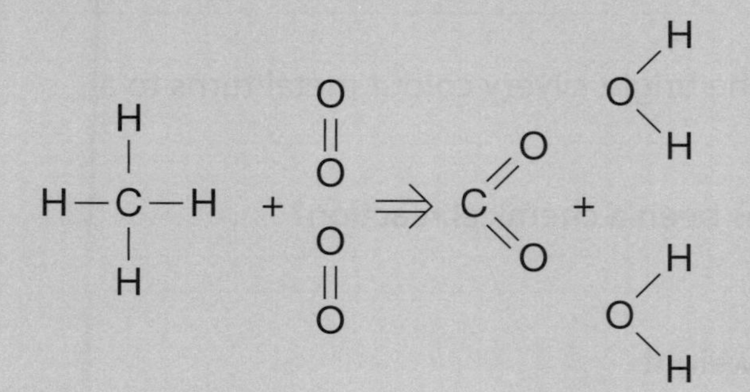

One way to view the reaction between methane and oxygen. Check that there are the same number of each kind of atom before and after the reaction.

USING CHEMISTRY

1 A chemical reaction that happens in your home involves burning natural gas in oxygen.

(a) Is this an endothermic reaction or an exothermic reaction?

____ 1 mark

(b) Explain your answer to part (a).

____ 1 mark

2 Plaster of Paris (calcium sulphate) can be used to hold limbs in place while broken bones mend. To make it, a dry powder is mixed with water. The mixture gets warm, and hardens into a white solid.

(a) Give **two** pieces of evidence that a chemical reaction has occurred.

____ 1 mark

(b) Is this an endothermic reaction or an exothermic reaction?

____ 1 mark

3 A bath with Epson salts dissolved in it can help you to relax. The active ingredient in Epson Salts is magnesium sulphate, $Mg\ SO_4$.
How many different elements are there in magnesium sulphate?

____ 1 mark

4 Baking powder is also known as sodium bicarbonate. The chemical term is sodium hydrogen carbonate.
When cakes are baked, the following reaction happens:

$2NaHCO_3 \rightarrow Na_2CO_3 + CO_2 + H_2O$

(a) How many different elements are there in baking soda?

____ 1 mark

(b) H_2O leaves the cake as a gas. Which gas?

____ 1 mark

(c) Na_2CO_3 is known as 'washing soda'. Suggest a reason why it is important not to add too much baking powder when you bake a cake.

____ 1 mark

5 A sample of magnesium is heated in air. The bright silvery colour metal turns to a white powder and gains weight.

(a) What evidence is there that there has been a chemical reaction?

____ 1 mark

(b) Explain why the sample has gained weight.

__________________________________ 1 mark

TOTAL

How did you score?

4 or less – try again!
5 – 7 – nearly there!
8 – 10 – well done!

ENERGY AND ELECTRICITY

Week 7
Wednesday

What you need to know

1. Know a range of useful energy transfers and transformations.
2. Know that electricity is used to transfer energy to do useful things.
3. Know how electricity is generated, and how this can impact on the environment.
4. Know how voltage is linked with the transfer of energy in a circuit.
5. Know how the voltage of a cell can change over time.
6. Know how to use the principle of conservation of energy to identify ways in which energy is dissipated during transfers (e.g. as heat or light).

WHAT IS ENERGY?

- Energy gives you the ability to do work.
- Some energy forms can be detected by our senses.
- Some energy is 'hidden' and can only be detected when it is transferred into visible forms.
- In any event, energy is conserved. However, it can be transferred into other forms.
- When energy is transferred, some is dissipated to the environment as heat.

Types of energy

chemical	kinetic (motion)
gravitational	heat
strain	light
electricity	sound
nuclear	

WHY IS ELECTRICITY SO IMPORTANT?

- Electricity is a versatile form of energy because:
  - it is relatively easy to transport around the country;
  - it can be converted into other forms (e.g. heat, light and movement);
  - it does not cause pollution where it is used.

HOW IS ELECTRICITY GENERATED?

- Most electricity is generated by spinning coils of wire rapidly in a magnetic field. The coils are made to spin using turbine blades through which hot gases pass. The hot gases are made by burning gas or generating steam.
- The waste products from burning fossil fuels contribute to problems like acid rain and global warming.

THINGS TO REMEMBER ABOUT ELECTRICITY

- The amount of electrical energy in a wire is indicated by the 'voltage'.
- As electricity passes through components, the voltage reduces. This happens because energy is converted from electrical into other types (e.g. heat) and leaves the wire.
- Chemical reactions can be used to produce electricity. This happens inside an electrical cell (sometimes called a battery).
- As the chemicals are used up in the reactions, the electrical energy that the cell produces gets less. As this happens the voltage of the cell reduces (the battery runs down).

ENERGY AND ELECTRICITY

1 (a) What kind of energy is stored in an electrical cell? ______________ 1 mark

(b) What kind of energy is produced by an electrical cell? ______________ 1 mark

2 Join each device to the correct energy change.

A electric motor
B loudspeaker
C light bulb
D microphone
E generator

1 sound → electricity + heat
2 electricity → motion + sound + heat
3 electricity → sound + heat
4 motion → electricity + heat
5 electricity → light + heat

5 marks

3 What is the principle of conservation of energy? ______________

______________ 1 mark

4 What are **two** problems of burning fossil fuels to generate electricity?

______________ 2 marks

5 'Electricity is a clean source of energy.'

(a) Is the statement above true or false? ______________ 1 mark

(b) Explain your answer to part (a). ______________

______________ 1 mark

6 Explain why electricity is a popular form of energy.

______________ 1 mark

7 Below are three ways that electrical energy can be produced.

A chemical energy → heat → motion of turbines → motion of coils → heat + electricity

B nuclear energy → heat → motion of turbines → motion of coils → heat + electricity

C kinetic energy of waves → motion of turbines → motion of coils → heat + electricity

(a) Which method is a 'renewable' way of generating electricity? ______________ 1 mark

(b) Which method involves using a nuclear reactor? ______________ 1 mark

(c) Which method involves burning fossil fuels? ______________ 1 mark

TOTAL [ ]

How did you score?
7 or less – try again!
8 – 12 – nearly there!
13 – 16 – well done!

GRAVITY AND SPACE

Week 7
Thursday

What you need to know

1. Know that there is a gravitational pull between all bodies.
2. Know that the amount of gravitational pull depends on the masses of bodies and the distance between them.
3. Know how the movement of planets around the Sun, and that of satellites around the Earth, is controlled by gravitation.
4. Know how artificial satellites are used to observe the Earth and provide information about the solar system and the universe.
5. Know how humans are trying to explore space.

GRAVITY

- Gravity is a force that acts between all masses in the universe, pulling them together.
- The more massive the objects, the greater the force of attraction.
- The closer the objects are to each other, the greater the force of attraction.
- Without gravity, the Moon would not orbit the Earth and the Earth would not orbit the Sun. Instead they would travel away into space.

ARTIFICIAL SATELLITES

- Artificial satellites are placed in orbit around the Earth by humans.
- Artificial satellites that orbit close to the Earth complete an orbit once every 90 minutes. Their orbit takes them over the North and South Poles.

- These satellites are used for:
  - weather prediction;
  - mapping the Earth;
  - spying;
  - vehicle navigation.

- Artificial satellites that orbit far from the Earth complete an orbit once every 24 hours. Their orbit is in line with the equator.

- These satellites are used for:
  - communications;
  - weather prediction.

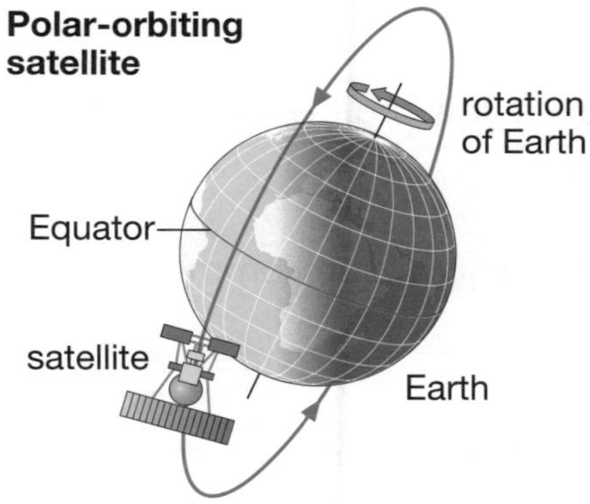

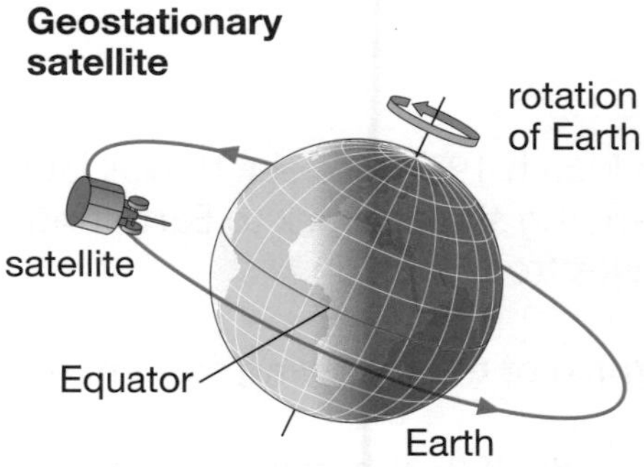

EXPLORING SPACE

- To explore space, engineers have made vehicles that can travel to the planets in our solar system. These vehicles can analyse the chemistry of planets and their atmospheres.
- It is more cost-effective and safer to use computer-controlled space vehicles instead of astronauts to explore the solar system.
- In addition to space probes, large telescopes on Earth and in orbit around the Earth collect images about more distant objects such as galaxies.

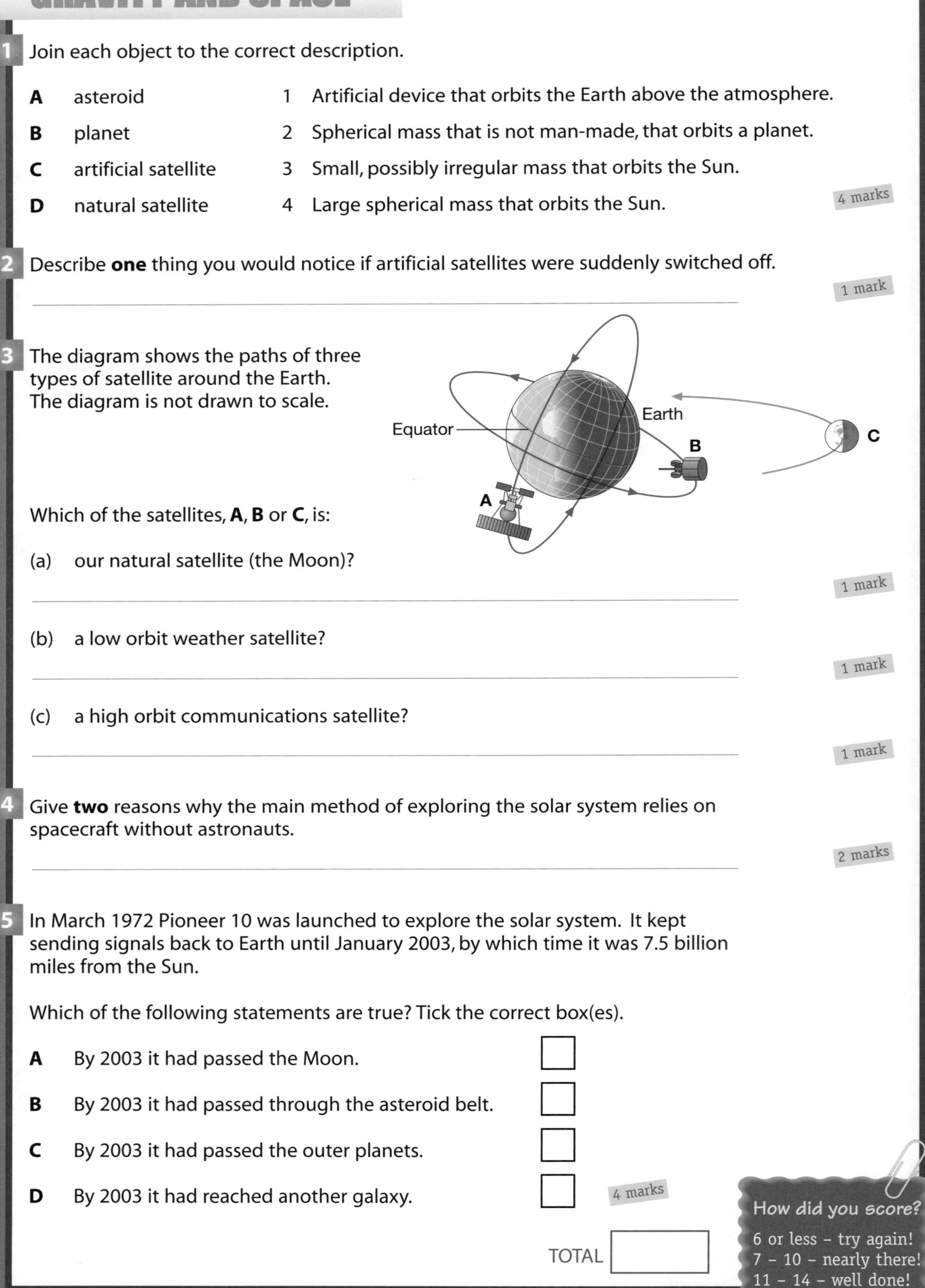

GRAVITY AND SPACE

1 Join each object to the correct description.

A	asteroid	1	Artificial device that orbits the Earth above the atmosphere.
B	planet	2	Spherical mass that is not man-made, that orbits a planet.
C	artificial satellite	3	Small, possibly irregular mass that orbits the Sun.
D	natural satellite	4	Large spherical mass that orbits the Sun.

4 marks

2 Describe **one** thing you would notice if artificial satellites were suddenly switched off.

______________________________ 1 mark

3 The diagram shows the paths of three types of satellite around the Earth. The diagram is not drawn to scale.

Which of the satellites, **A**, **B** or **C**, is:

(a) our natural satellite (the Moon)?

______________________________ 1 mark

(b) a low orbit weather satellite?

______________________________ 1 mark

(c) a high orbit communications satellite?

______________________________ 1 mark

4 Give **two** reasons why the main method of exploring the solar system relies on spacecraft without astronauts.

______________________________ 2 marks

5 In March 1972 Pioneer 10 was launched to explore the solar system. It kept sending signals back to Earth until January 2003, by which time it was 7.5 billion miles from the Sun.

Which of the following statements are true? Tick the correct box(es).

A By 2003 it had passed the Moon. ☐

B By 2003 it had passed through the asteroid belt. ☐

C By 2003 it had passed the outer planets. ☐

D By 2003 it had reached another galaxy. ☐

4 marks

TOTAL ☐

How did you score?
6 or less – try again!
7 – 10 – nearly there!
11 – 14 – well done!

SPEED AND STREAMLINING

Week 7
Friday

What you need to know

1. Know how to use the concept of speed.
2. Know how to consider the relationship between forces (including balanced forces) on an object and its movement.
3. Know how to study the effects of water and air resistance on speed and how streamlining reduces these effects.
4. Know how to use ideas of balanced and unbalanced forces to explain the movement of falling objects.

HOW A FORCE AFFECTS AN OBJECT

- An object will stay at rest, or keep moving in a straight line at a steady speed unless an unbalanced force acts on it.
- If an unbalanced force acts on the object, it will either change its speed or its direction – or both.
- The less mass the object has, the more a given force will affect its motion.

STREAMLINING

- When travelling through air or water, there are forces that resist motion. These forces are called drag. The greater the speed, the greater the amount of drag.
- To keep moving at a steady speed, the engines must provide a forward force that matches the drag.
- Drag can be reduced if the object is streamlined. This allows the vehicle to travel faster before the drag and forward forces match.

Case study

Before opening the parachute, a skydiver travels at a high speed towards the ground. Their weight is matched by the air resistance, so they fall at a steady speed.

Once the parachute is opened, they are less streamlined. Their weight is still matched by the air resistance, but because they are larger, this balance of forces occurs at a slower speed.

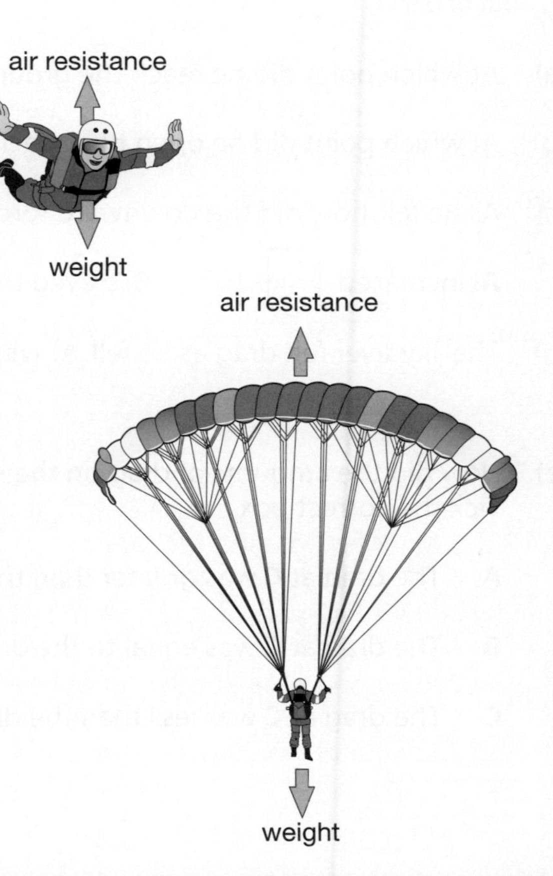

SPEED AND STREAMLINING

1 Racing cyclists crouch towards their handlebars when they are racing. Why do they do this?

____ 1 mark

2 A snowflake falls at a slower speed than a raindrop. Give **two** reasons why.

____ 2 marks

3 A rower turns their oar as they row, so the end of it is horizontal as it passes through the air and vertical as it goes through the water. Explain why the rower rotates the oar in this way. Make sure you use the word **drag** in your answer.

direction of pull
direction of boat movement
direction of boat
oar beneath water
oar on top of water

1 mark

4 The graph below shows the speed of a skydiver as he fell to ground.

speed
A
B
C
D
E
F
time
diver jumps out of plane

(a) At which point did he reach the ground? ______________________ 1 mark

(b) At which point did he open his parachute? ______________________ 1 mark

(c) As he fell, how did the downward force on him change? Tick the correct box.

A increased ☐ **B** stayed the same ☐ **C** decreased ☐ 1 mark

(d) The skydiver felt drag as he fell. At what **two** points was the drag zero?

____ 2 marks

(e) How did the amounts of drag on the skydiver compare at points **C** and **E**? Tick the correct box.

A The drag at **C** was greater than the drag at **E**. ☐

B The drag at **C** was equal to the drag at **E**. ☐

C The drag at **C** was less than the drag at **E**. ☐

1 mark

TOTAL ☐

How did you score?
4 or less – try again!
5 – 7 – nearly there!
8 – 10 – well done!

PRESSURE AND MOMENTS

Week 8
Monday

What you need to know

1. Know the principle of moments.
2. Know how **levers** operate.
3. Understand how to calculate the turning effect of a force.
4. Know examples of levers from the human body.
5. Know how to calculate pressure with solids and describe applications of this in everyday appliances.
6. Know about hydrostatic pressure in fluids and be able to describe an application, e.g. hydraulic jack.

FLOATING

- Objects that float displace water and feel an upward force called **upthrust.**
- For an object that is floating:

upthrust = weight of the object = weight of liquid displaced

LEVERS AND MOMENTS

- The turning effect of a force is called its **moment.**
- The greater the distance a force acts from a pivot, the more turning effect it has.
- The moment of a force is calculated using the formula:

moment = force x distance (**Note:** the force must act at 90° to the pivot)

- If there are two forces that are tending to rotate an object, they will balance if their moments are equal. This is called the principle of moments.

PRESSURE

- A force acting on a small area produces a large **pressure.**
- Pressure is defined as:

pressure = force/area.

- Pressure can be reduced by increasing the area over which the force acts.

FORCES AND LIQUIDS

- Liquids cannot be easily compressed, so applying a pressure at one point produces an equal pressure at every other point.
- By using wide and narrow containers that are linked, it is possible to produce a large force (in the wide container) by applying a small force (in the narrow container).

THE NARROW CONTAINER

- A piston in the narrow container will move a long way but the piston in a connected wide container will only move a short distance.

PRESSURE AND MOMENTS

1 Creatures that live on mud have wide feet. Describe the advantage of this.

1 mark

2 Needles used to inject patients have sharp points. Explain the advantage of using a sharp needle rather than a blunt one.

1 mark

3 The diagram shows a simple mobile that is designed to be hung in a child's bedroom. All of the fish weigh the same.

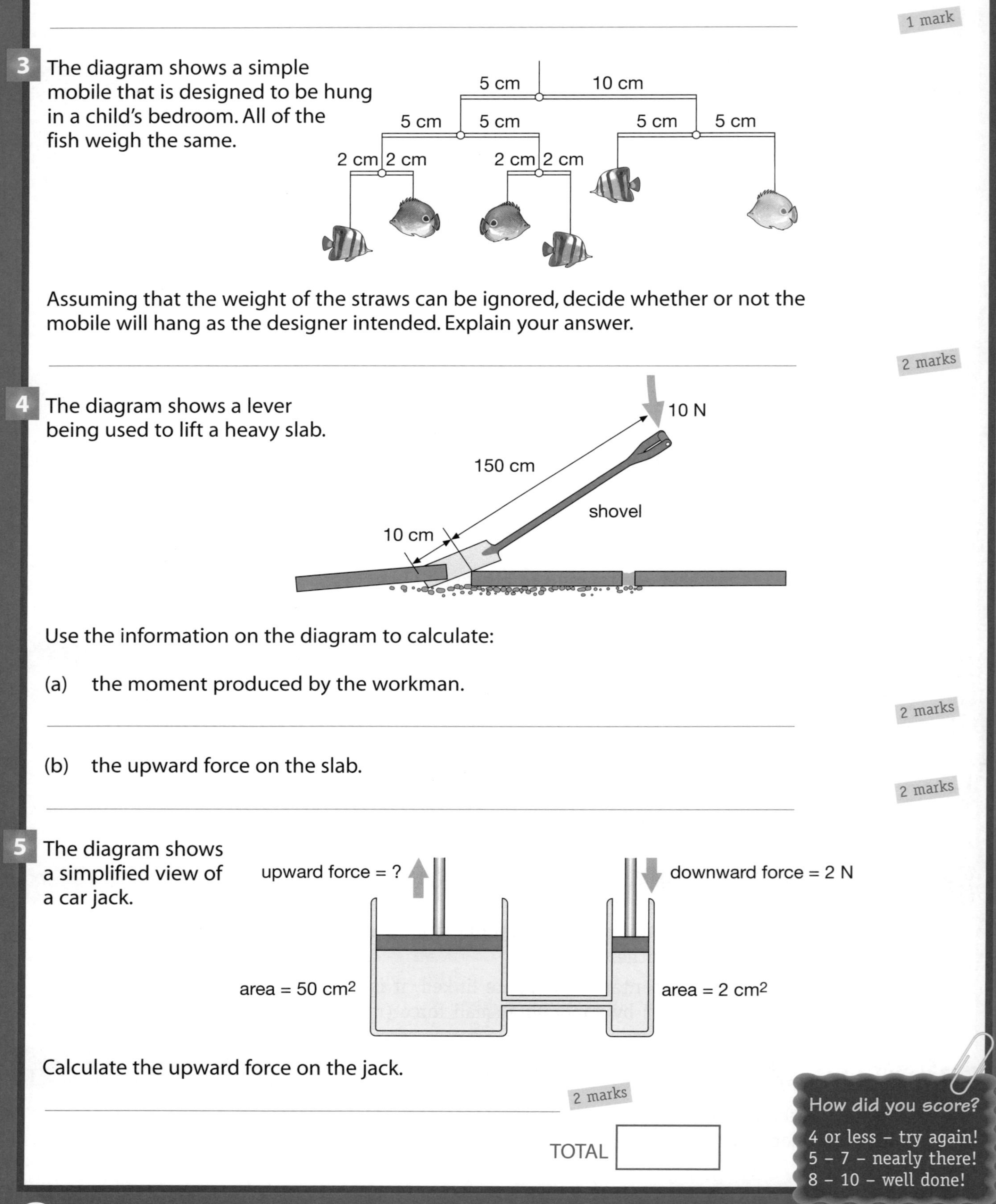

Assuming that the weight of the straws can be ignored, decide whether or not the mobile will hang as the designer intended. Explain your answer.

2 marks

4 The diagram shows a lever being used to lift a heavy slab.

Use the information on the diagram to calculate:

(a) the moment produced by the workman.

2 marks

(b) the upward force on the slab.

2 marks

5 The diagram shows a simplified view of a car jack.

Calculate the upward force on the jack.

2 marks

TOTAL

How did you score?

4 or less – try again!
5 – 7 – nearly there!
8 – 10 – well done!

SCIENTIFIC QUESTIONS

Week 8
Tuesday

What you need to know

1. Know which kind of questions are suitable for scientific enquiry.
2. Know how to use a variety of strategies to answer scientific questions of different kinds.
3. Know how to plan and set targets for a piece of work.

WHAT IS A SCIENTIFIC QUESTION?

- Scientific questions can be answered by experiments that are repeatable and open to scrutiny. They can be used to:
  - make decisions (Which methods of farming encourage biodiversity?);
  - refine measurements (What is the speed of light to 9 significant figures?);
  - develop models (Does a wave model or a particle model explain the behaviour of light?).
- Non-scientific questions cannot be answered using experiments:

Examples

Personal taste: "What would you like to eat for dinner?"
Artistic: "Is this sculpture beautiful?"
Religious: "What is the nature of heaven?"
Moral: "Is euthanasia immoral?"

DESIGNING THE EXPERIMENT

- Expectations of the *answer* to a scientific question are necessary in order to design the *experiment*.
- Predicting the values that will be collected helps us to choose the most appropriate apparatus.

Expectations

"I think 1 ml of this drug will make a person's heart beat more regularly, but 10 ml might make the heart stop."

"The catalyst will probably work best at a high temperature and pressure. I will design my apparatus to cope with these conditions."

"I think light travels very quickly, so I will design my apparatus with this in mind."

- You need to decide which variable you will set, and which other variable you will measure. These are called the independent and dependent variables.

The value for the independent variable is set by the experimenter.

The dependent variable is measured to see how it changes as the independent variable is changed.

- It is also important to decide on the kinds of readings you will take, and how many. This is especially important if an experiment is likely to take a long time and use expensive resources.

Example

It may take eight years to prove a new drug has the effect you want and is safe to use. It is important to decide in advance of the drug-trials how much evidence needs to be gathered.

SCIENTIFIC QUESTIONS

1 Which of the questions below could be answered by carrying out a scientific enquiry? Tick the correct boxes.

A How many centimetres thick should the concrete be to support the road safely? ☐

B How are you feeling today? ☐

C Which is the most efficient catalyst for producing ammonia? ☐

D Where shall we go for our holiday? ☐

E Is vivisection wrong? ☐

F Is low sulphur fuel better for the environment than regular fuel? ☐

G Is a copy of the Bible in a museum from the 5th or 10th centuries? ☐

H Was Isaac Newton or Leonardo Da Vinci the best scientist? ☐

I Which is the most entertaining football team? ☐

9 marks

2 Read the predictions below and then answer the questions.

A "I think hot water will dissolve more sugar than cold water."

B "I think that water that has a temperature of 40°C will dissolve twice as much sugar as water at 20°C."

C "I think that 100 ml of water at a temperature of 20°C will dissolve 10 g of sugar, and 100 ml of water at a temperature of 40°C will dissolve twice as much."

(a) Which prediction helps the scientist to select the sensitivity of the weighing device to use?

______________________________ 1 mark

(b) Which predictions help the scientist to select the kind of thermometer to use?

______________________________ 1 mark

(c) Which is the **least** useful prediction for helping the scientist choose the apparatus for the experiment?

______________________________ 1 mark

(d) Complete the table below with values that are consistent with the pattern suggested by prediction **C**.

Temperature of water	°C	10	20	40	80
Amount of sugar dissolved	g	10			

3 marks

(e) Explain why it would be unwise to make predictions for much higher or much lower temperatures.

______________________________ 1 mark

TOTAL ☐

How did you score?
7 or less – try again!
8 – 12 – nearly there!
13 – 16 – well done!

PLAN AND DESIGN EXPERIMENTS

Week 8
Wednesday

What you need to know

1 Know how to select apparatus and a data-collection technique.

SELECTING APPARATUS

- The apparatus chosen for an experiment depends on the type of data being collected and how precise the measurements need to be. There is no point in using a stopwatch to time an experiment that lasts for a week.

FAIR TESTS

- Fair tests are important if you are trying to compare two (or more) situations.
- Fair tests involve keeping all variables the same in all the tests – except for the variables you are investigating.
- In biology, identical twins are often used for fair tests.

REPEATING OBSERVATIONS

- If the data that is to be collected tends to vary over time (such as how many animals live in an area), repeat readings allow an average value to be calculated.
- Repeat readings reduce the effect of small random variations.

SECONDARY DATA

- During an experiment, scientists collect some data themselves and use some data from other sources, such as books or journals.
- If secondary data is used, it is important that it comes from a reliable source.

PRECISION AND ACCURACY

- Accurate data contains no errors. Accurate data is close to the 'true' value.
- Precise data has many significant figures.
- Ideally, an experiment would be both accurate and precise.

The precision of your readings is determined by the apparatus used. (If your metre rule only has markings in cm, you cannot measure to the nearest mm.)

The accuracy of your readings is determined by the apparatus and you. (If the metre rule has been calibrated wrongly or you are careless, the readings will not be accurate.)

PLAN AND DESIGN EXPERIMENTS

1 In comparison experiments, making sure it is a 'fair test' is vital.
For each of the following experiments, give **two** variables you would control to make sure the experiment was fair.

(a) Stretching wires made from different metals, to compare the strength of the metals.

_______________ 2 marks

(b) Comparing the effectiveness of two soluble weedkillers in killing ground elder.

_______________ 2 marks

(c) Finding out if a drug to lower blood pressure is effective.

_______________ 2 marks

(d) Finding out how much energy is saved by putting loft insulation into a house.

_______________ 2 marks

(e) Finding out which kind of cell keeps a torch lit longest.

_______________ 2 marks

(f) Finding out the effect of temperature on the rate at which yeast produces carbon dioxide when in a sugar solution.

_______________ 2 marks

2 The speed of light has been measured as: $2.997\ 924\ 58 \times 10^8$ m/s.

(a) A student carries out an experiment and says:
"On the evidence of my experiment, the speed of light is roughly 3×10^8 m/s."

(i) Was their experiment accurate? _______________ 1 mark

(ii) Was their value precise? _______________ 1 mark

(b) Another student carries out the same experiment and says:
"On the evidence of my experiment, the speed of light is $1.597\ 924\ 580\ 5 \times 10^8$ m/s."

(i) Was their experiment accurate? _______________ 1 mark

(ii) Was their value precise? _______________ 1 mark

3 Explain why it is often sensible to take repeat readings in an experiment, even if you have taken careful measurements.

_______________ 2 marks

4 What are 'secondary data sources' and why are they useful for scientists?

_______________ 2 marks

TOTAL

How did you score?
9 or less – try again!
10 – 14 – nearly there!
15 – 20 – well done!

OBTAIN AND PRESENT EVIDENCE

Week 8 Thursday

What you need to know

1. Know ways to present data to show patterns or trends.
2. Know how to use patterns or trends to make further predictions.
3. Know how to recognise data that does not fit a pattern or trend.

PRESENTING DATA

- Raw data is difficult to interpret. It usually needs to be presented in an appropriate way and manipulated mathematically.
- The purpose of graphing data is to:
  - look for patterns in the data;
  - predict values outside the range of readings (extrapolate);
  - predict missing values within the range of readings (interpolate).
- It is possible to use:
  - line graphs;
  - pie charts;
  - bar charts.

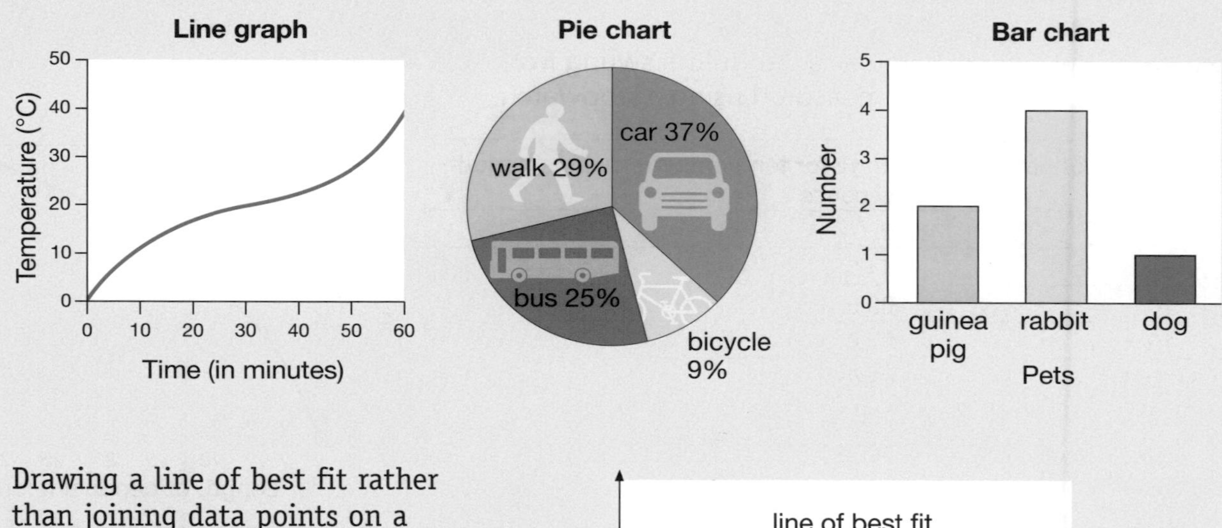

- Drawing a line of best fit rather than joining data points on a line graph:
  - shows a trend or pattern more clearly;
  - means that small errors in readings can be ignored;
  - means that anomalous results can be identified.

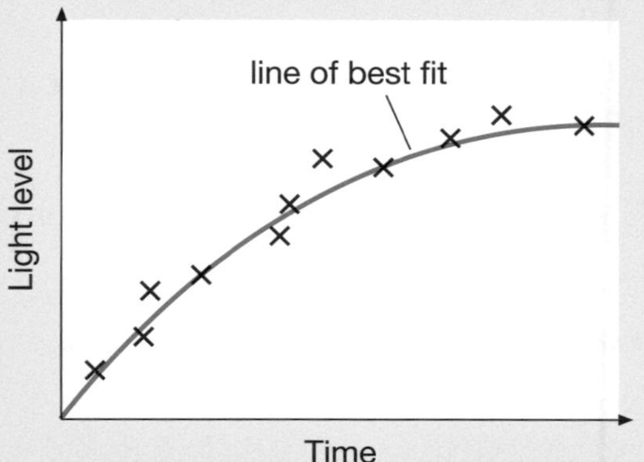

MANIPULATING DATA

- Common ways of manipulating data include:
  - calculating averages;
  - calculating correlations.

OBTAIN AND PRESENT EVIDENCE

1 The data below was collected as water cooled in an open container.
The data has been plotted and a line of best fit has been drawn.

Time minutes	**Temperature** °C
0	100
5	89
10	79
15	70
20	82
25	56
30	49

(a) Identify a result that appears to be **anomalous** and explain why you have selected it.

2 marks

(b) Predict the temperature after 7 minutes. ______ 1 mark

(c) Predict the temperature after 32 minutes. ______ 1 mark

(d) Explain why taking repeat readings would **not** increase accuracy in this experiment.

1 mark

2 The data below was collected as a pendulum swung from side to side. The time for 10 complete swings was measured using a stopwatch.

Length of pendulum cm	**Time for ten complete swings period** seconds
0	0
5	44.8
10	63.5
15	97.6
20	89.8
25	100.4
30	109.8

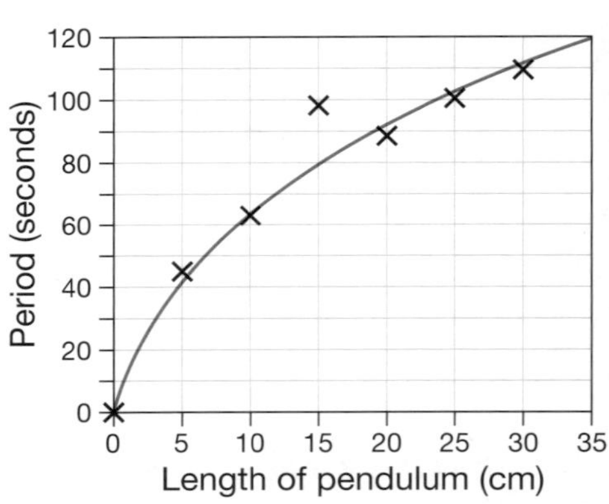

(a) Identify a result that appears to be **anomalous** and explain why you have selected it.

2 marks

(b) Predict the time for ten swings of a pendulum that is 7 cm long.

1 mark

(c) Predict the time for ten swings of a pendulum that is 32 cm long.

1 mark

(d) Explain why timing 10 swings was more sensible than timing a single swing.

1 mark

(e) Explain why taking repeat readings **could** improve accuracy in this experiment.

1 mark

TOTAL

How did you score?
5 or less – try again!
6 – 8 – nearly there!
9 – 11 – well done!

CONSIDER AND EVALUATE EVIDENCE

Week 8
Friday

What you need to know

1. Know how to judge the strength of the **evidence** in relation to the question investigated.
2. Know how to compare different investigative methods.

COINCIDENCES HAPPEN

- Sometimes when you meet people you are surprised by similarities between you. Perhaps you both have the same middle name, or both your birthdays are in October.
- Remember: coincidences happen. It would be *very* surprising if coincidences *never* happened.
- Coincidences are a problem for scientists. For example: how can we be sure a drug really did have an effect and that the effect was not just a coincidence?
- Experiments with important results need to be repeated – ideally by someone who was not involved in the first experiment – so we are more confident that what happened was not a coincidence.

DEALING WITH DATA THAT DOES NOT FIT THE PATTERN

- Some data may not fit the general pattern because of:
  - human error;
  - equipment malfunction.

  However, *we should not ignore any result without a good reason.*
- Four reasons for an anomalous result:
  - all the data is correct and something special happens at this value;
  - all the data that fits the pattern is *correct* and data that does not fit is *incorrect;*
  - the anomalous value is *correct* and the other data is *not correct;*
  - none of the data is reliable. The whole experiment was poor.

  We should repeat the experiment to check the anomalous value and also to check other values close to it.

HOW CAN WE BE SURE?

- Our knowledge of the universe is continually being refined. Science tries to make this process open to scrutiny, so other people can check scientific claims.
- When we make a scientific claim:
  - the claim must be supported by **evidence**;
  - the evidence must be available for other scientists to view;
  - the record of how the experiment was carried out must be detailed enough for another scientist to repeat the experiment.
- As more scientists carry out experiments where results are consistent with each other, confidence grows. However, scientists should always try to keep an open mind.

CONSIDER AND EVALUATE EVIDENCE

1 You meet someone who was born in the same month as you.

(a) What is the chance that someone you meet will have the same birth month as yours?

1 mark

(b) Twenty-four people attend a party. Predict how many people at the party might have the same birth month as yours.

1 mark

2 Explain what is meant by the phrase 'anomalous reading'.

1 mark

3 Describe the most appropriate way to deal with an anomalous reading.

1 mark

4 Explain why it is unwise to just ignore an anomalous reading.

1 mark

5 The Moon normally looks pale grey from Earth. A friend says: "A friend of mine was looking at the Moon a few nights ago and it seemed to turn a funny colour!"

(a) How should you view such a claim? Tick the correct box.

A Believe the claim ☐ **B** Be sceptical ☐ **C** Ignore the claim ☐

1 mark

(b) Explain your answer to part (a).

1 mark

(c) What **three** questions should you ask to clarify the claim?

3 marks

6 A friend says: "There's this brilliant diet that this doctor invented. You eat as much as you like of one kind of food for a week and you lose loads of weight!"

(a) How should you view such a claim? Tick the correct box.

A Believe the claim ☐ **B** Be sceptical ☐ **C** Ignore the claim ☐

1 mark

(b) Explain your answer to part (a).

1 mark

(c) What **three** questions should you ask to clarify the claim?

3 marks

TOTAL ☐

How did you score?

6 or less – try again!
7 – 10 – nearly there!
11 – 15 – well done!

PRACTICE TEST

1. (a) Which **two** cells pass on information from parents to their children?
Tick the correct boxes.

bone cell ☐ egg cell ☐ cheek cell ☐

muscle cell ☐ sperm cell ☐ red blood cell ☐

1 mark

(b) Which organ system produces the cells you selected in part (a)?
Tick the correct box.

respiratory system ☐ **digestive system** ☐

reproductive system ☐ **circulatory system** ☐

1 mark

(c) Some characteristics of a person are inherited from their parents. Others are dependent on the environment in which a person grows up.
Describe **one** characteristic of a person that is due to the genetic information they inherit from their parents.

____

1 mark

maximum 3 marks

2. Bill and Anju investigated how pupils in their class were the same and different.
First they measured the length of each pupil's foot.

(a) Explain why each pupil should keep their toes uncurled while it is being measured.

____

____

1 mark

(b) The bar chart below shows their results.

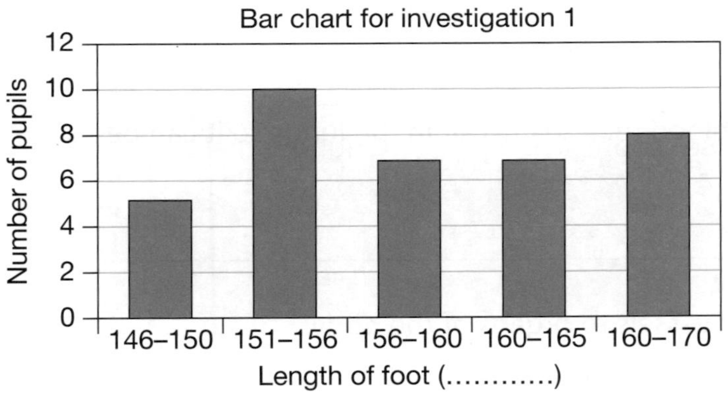

Bar chart for investigation 1

Number of pupils: 0, 2, 4, 6, 8, 10, 12

146–150, 151–156, 156–160, 160–165, 160–170

Length of foot (............)

1 mark

(i) What units of measurement did they use?

(ii) Describe the mistake they made in the way they grouped the foot lengths in their bar chart.

____

1 mark

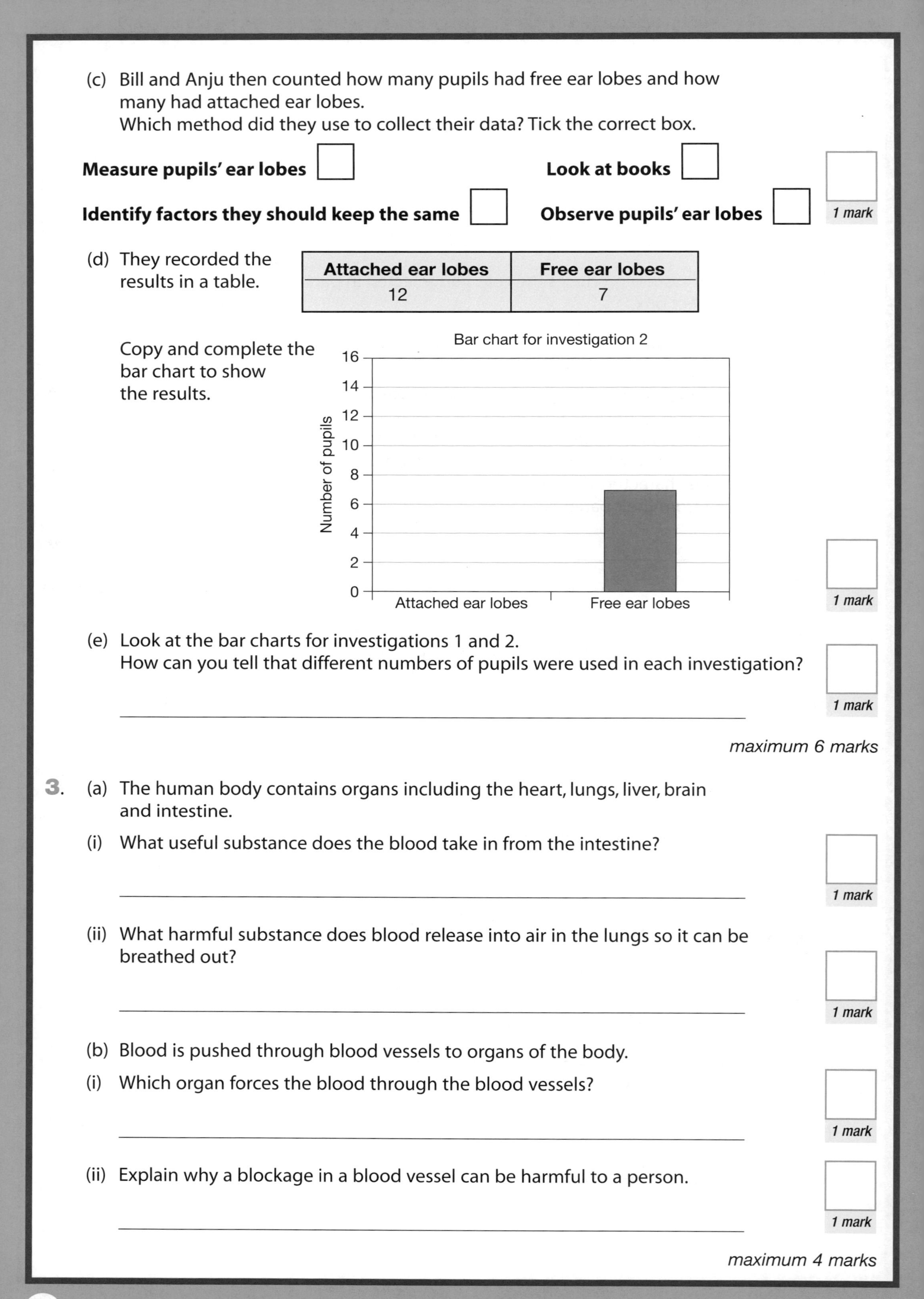

(c) Bill and Anju then counted how many pupils had free ear lobes and how many had attached ear lobes.
Which method did they use to collect their data? Tick the correct box.

Measure pupils' ear lobes ☐ **Look at books** ☐

Identify factors they should keep the same ☐ **Observe pupils' ear lobes** ☐

1 mark

(d) They recorded the results in a table.

Attached ear lobes	Free ear lobes
12	7

Copy and complete the bar chart to show the results.

Bar chart for investigation 2

Number of pupils

16
14
12
10
8
6
4
2
0

Attached ear lobes
Free ear lobes

1 mark

(e) Look at the bar charts for investigations 1 and 2.
How can you tell that different numbers of pupils were used in each investigation?

____

1 mark

maximum 6 marks

3. (a) The human body contains organs including the heart, lungs, liver, brain and intestine.

(i) What useful substance does the blood take in from the intestine?

____

1 mark

(ii) What harmful substance does blood release into air in the lungs so it can be breathed out?

____

1 mark

(b) Blood is pushed through blood vessels to organs of the body.

(i) Which organ forces the blood through the blood vessels?

____

1 mark

(ii) Explain why a blockage in a blood vessel can be harmful to a person.

____

1 mark

maximum 4 marks

4. A space probe on the planet Mars identifies an unknown material and sends back the following information to scientists on Earth.

It is not a good conductor of electricity.
It is not a good conductor of heat.
It is red in colour.
It is not magnetic.
It is not very reactive.

(a) Which **two** properties indicate that the unknown material is probably **not** a metal?

____

____

2 marks

(b) The material is crushed and mixed with water to find out if it is a pure substance. Explain how the results of this process can show if it is a pure substance or an impure substance.

____

____

2 marks

(c) The water turns red and there is a solid left at the bottom. Give the name of the method that should be used to separate the solids from the liquid.

____

1 mark

(d) The red solution is left and after several days red crystals are seen. Explain what has happened to the water.

____

1 mark

maximum 6 marks

5. (a) When a sound wave reaches your eardrum it vibrates.

(i) Describe what happens to bone **A** when this happens.

____

1 mark

(ii) Some people have a disease that makes the bones in their ears very soft and they even break. Give **one** reason why people with this disease cannot hear very well.

____

1 mark

(b) A scientist found the lowest and highest frequencies that five living things are able to hear.

living thing	lowest frequency (Hz)	highest frequency (Hz)
human	20	18 000
bat	1000	80 000
cat	20	64 000
dog	20	50 000
elephant	8	20 000

(i) Which **three** living things in the table can hear a frequency of 50 000 Hz?

____

1 mark

(ii) From the table choose the living creature that can hear the smallest range of frequencies.

____

1 mark

maximum 4 marks

6. Bill and Betty want to find out which type of CD case protects their CDs best.

Clam case

Crystal case

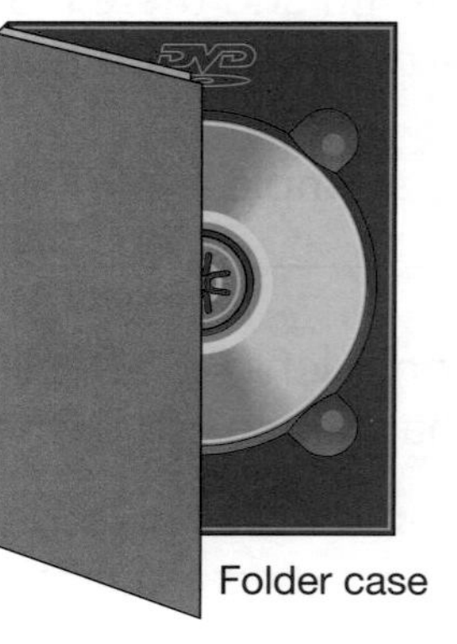

Folder case

To do this, they could do **A** or **B** below.

A
- Use three CD cases and three CDs.

B
- Collect three different CD cases.
- Collect three CDs to place inside the cases.
- Drop a 100 g mass from a height of 1 m onto each case.
- Examine the CD inside each case.
- Increase the size of the mass until the CD inside the case is damaged so that it will not play any more.

(a) Explain why plan **B** is better than **A**.

____

1 mark

(b) Describe **one** safety precaution they should take when carrying out this investigation.

____

1 mark

(c) Bill and Betty could choose between different shaped masses.
Explain why a spherical mass is likely to produce a fairer test.

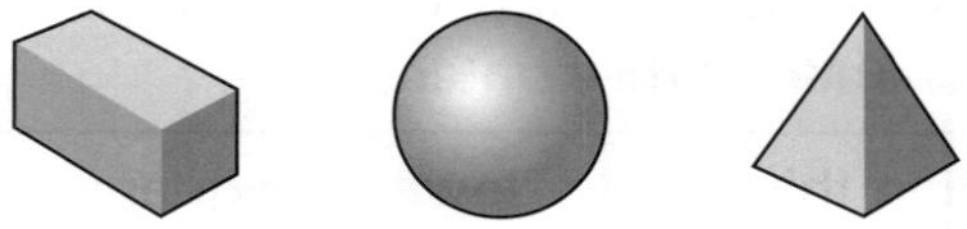

____

1 mark

(d)

CD case	Mass to damage the CD
Clam	500 g
Crystal	300 g
Folder	400 g

(i) Which part of the investigation – explanations, results, plans or conclusions – was recorded in the table?

____

1 mark

(ii) Write down the three CD cases in order of the protection they gave to the CD.

most protective **least protective**

______________ ______________ ______________

1 mark

maximum 5 marks

7. The drawing shows a simple circuit to test different materials.

Circuit 1

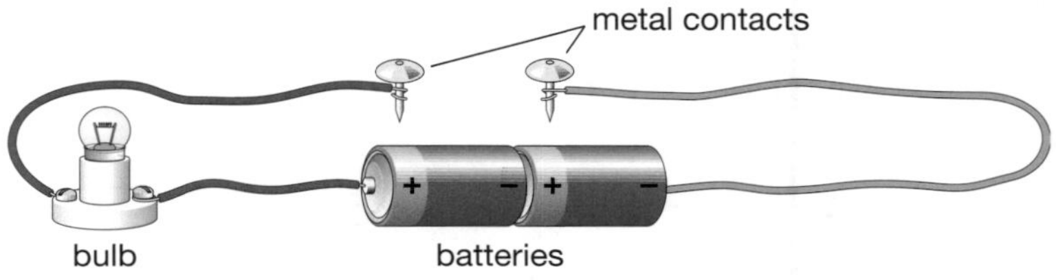

(a) A piece of aluminium was placed across the contacts and the bulb lit.
Explain why this made the bulb light.

____

1 mark

(b) A piece of paper placed across the contacts did not make the bulb light.
Explain why this did not make the bulb light.

____

1 mark

(c) Look carefully at Circuit 2 and Circuit 3.

Circuit 2

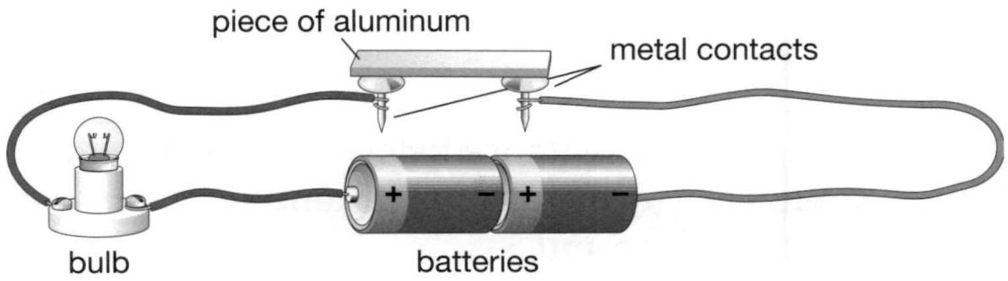

Circuit 3

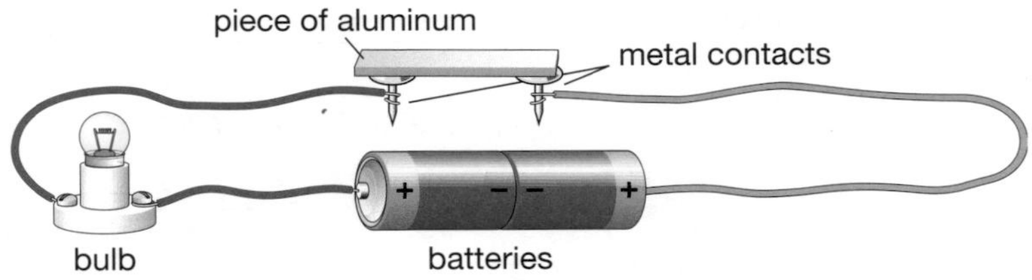

(i) Explain why the bulb in Circuit 2 did not light – even when aluminium was placed across the contacts.

____

1 mark

(ii) Explain why the bulb in Circuit 3 did not light – even when aluminium was placed across the contacts.

____

1 mark

(d) After using Circuit 1 for several weeks, it stopped working. Give a reason why it stopped working, even though it was connected correctly.

____

1 mark

maximum 5 marks

8. The drawing shows a child swinging from **A** to **B** to **C** and back again.

A

B

C

(a) At which point(s) does the child have no kinetic energy? Give the correct letter(s).

____

2 marks

(b) At which point(s) does the child have most gravitational potential energy? Give the correct letter(s).

____

2 marks

(c) At which point(s) does the child have some kinetic energy and the least gravitational potential energy? Give the correct letter(s).

____

2 marks

(d) What force causes the swing to move from **A** to **B**?

____

1 mark

(e) Name **one** force that acts to stop the child from swinging.

____

1 mark

(f) Complete the sentence below by selecting from the following list.

chemical	**gravitational potential**	**kinetic**
light	**sound**	**thermal**

When the swing moves from **A** to **B**, most of the ____________________ energy

turns into ____________________ energy. Some energy is also transferred

into ____________________ energy.

3 marks

maximum 11 marks

Total Score

GLOSSARY

acid A chemical that turns litmus paper red – it can often dissolve things that water cannot.
adaptation A feature of a living organism that helps it to survive, e.g. the zebra's stripes are an adaptation that makes it difficult to see in the wild and so protects it from lions.
aerobic respiration Aerobic respiration breaks down glucose using oxygen to make energy available for chemical reactions in cells.
alkali A substance which makes a solution that turns red litmus paper blue.
antibodies Chemicals produced by cells to attack invading microorganisms.
artery A blood vessel carrying blood away from the heart under high pressure.
atom The smallest part of an element. Atoms consist of negatively-charged electrons flying around a positively-charged nucleus.
balanced diet A diet containing a mixture of all of the food groups needed to keep you healthy in the right amounts.
carnivore An animal that eats other animals.
cell The smallest parts of a living thing. Cells usually have a nucleus and cytoplasm and a range of other parts. Cells of some types of microorganisms do not have a proper nucleus.
change of state A change of state is a change from a gas to a liquid or back again or from a solid to a liquid or back.
chemical change / reaction A change that occurs when a number of substances react together to produce new substances.
chlorophyll A chemical in some plants that allows them to use energy from sunlight to make sugar.
classification Arranging things into sets according to the features that they have in common.
compound Compounds are groups of atoms bound together, in fixed proportions, by chemical bonds. Compounds have different chemical and physical properties to the elements that they contain.
conduction Movement of energy as heat (or electricity) through a substance without the substance itself moving.
consumer Organisms in an ecosystem that use up organic matter produced by other organisms. All animals are consumers.
convection Movement of a heated substance which carries energy with it as heat.
current The flow of electrical charge through an electrical circuit.
cytoplasm The living material inside a cell that is not in the nucleus.
displacement reaction A reaction where one chemical, usually a metal, is forced out of a compound by another chemical - also usually a metal.
eclipse An eclipse occurs when one object moves in front of another.
electromagnet A coil of copper wire, often surrounding an iron bar, that produces a magnetic field when electricity flows through the copper wire.
element A substance that cannot be split into anything simpler by chemical means.
energy Energy is the ability of a system to do something (work). We detect energy by the effect it has on the things around us, for example, heating them up, moving them, etc.
enzyme Special proteins found in living organisms that speed up the rate of a chemical reaction.
erosion Erosion occurs when the surface of the land is worn away by particles of rock carried by wind, water or ice.
evaporation When a liquid changes to a gas it evaporates. We use the word boiling when the liquid is evaporating as quickly as possible.
evidence Evidence includes all the results and data collected from investigations. People should agree about evidence even if they disagree about what a piece of evidence means.
fertilise When male and female gametes join together, for example, pollen and ovules in flowers or sperm and eggs in mammals.
fetus The baby growing inside the womb of the mother.
food chain A simple diagram using arrows to show the feeding relationships between some plants and animals.
force A force is a push or pull which is able to change the velocity or shape of a body. Forces only exist between bodies. Every force that acts on a body causes an equal and opposite reaction from the body.
forcemeter A device for measuring the size of a force. It is often called a spring balance because weight is a force.
formula (chemical) A shorthand way to show the type and amount of elements present in a compound.
fossil fuel A fuel like coal, oil and natural gas formed by the decay of dead living things over millions of years.
friction Friction is a force that acts between two surfaces in contact with each other. It tends to prevent or slow down movement by the two surfaces.
gas All substances are solids, liquids or gases. A gas has no fixed shape and will expand to fill all of the space available in the container where it is stored.
gravity The force of attraction between two bodies caused by their mass. The force of gravity produced by a body depends on its mass - the larger the mass the larger the force.
habitat The area where an organism lives.
haemoglobin A complex chemical found in red blood cells that can combine with oxygen to help transport it around the body. Haemoglobin is a protein and contains an iron atom.
herbivore An animal that eats plants.
igneous rock Rocks formed from solidified molten magma.
immunisation Giving someone a vaccination which protects them against an infectious disease.
indicator A chemical that changes colour in acid and alkaline solutions. Indicators are used to find out the pH of a solution.
insoluble A substance that will not dissolve. Something that is insoluble in water may be soluble in other liquids.
insulator A substance that will not let energy pass through it easily. You can have insulators for heat, electricity or sound.
levers A rigid bar that balances around a fulcrum. If you push down on one end of a lever, the other end moves up. Levers are often used to magnify the effective force.

liquid All substances are solids, liquids or gases. A liquid has a fixed volume but will change shape to lie in the bottom of any container that holds it.
magnetic field An area where a magnetic force can be felt.
mammal A type of animal that has fur, gives birth to live young and feeds them on milk produced by the female.
menstrual cycle The cycle of changes in the human female reproductive organs including egg maturation, release and menstruation. It typically lasts anything from four to six weeks.
metal A substance that is shiny when pure, can be beaten into sheets or drawn into wires. Metals usually have quite high melting points and conduct heat and electricity well.
metamorphic rock Metamorphic rock forms when heat and pressure changes the characteristics of an existing rock.
microorganisms Very small living things. You need a microscope to see microorganisms. Most are harmless, some are useful and some cause serious illnesses.
mixture A mixture contains at least two different substances. Some mixtures are easy to separate but others are very difficult to split up into their different components.
molecule A group of atoms joined together by chemical links.
moment The moment of a force acting on one side of a balanced bar is the force multiplied by the distance to the pivot.
neutralisation A reaction between an acid and an alkali to produce a neutral solution.
Newton The unit of force. An apple exerts a force of about 1 Newton on your hand if you hold it out in front of you.
non-metal An element that is not a metal. Non-metals are a very varied group and include solids, liquids and gases.
nucleus The control centre of the cell. The nucleus is surrounded by a membrane that separates it from the rest of the cell. Many microorganisms do not have a proper nucleus.
opaque Opaque objects will not let light through so they make a shadow, for example black paper is opaque.
organ A body part containing a number of different cell types.
ovulation The release of an egg from the ovary.
oxygen A colourless gas with no smell that makes up about 20% of the air.
pH scale The range of levels of acidity or alkalinity. A pH of 7 is neutral. A pH below 7 is acid and the lower it goes the more acid it becomes. A pH above 7 is alkaline.
photosynthesis The production, in green plants, of sugar and oxygen from carbon dioxide and water using light as an external energy source.
predator Animals that hunt and kill other animals.
pressure The force acting on a surface divided by the area of the surface. It is measured in Newtons per square metre (N/m^2).
prey Animals that are hunted by other animals.
producer An organism that makes organic material. Green plants are sometimes called primary producers because they use energy in sunlight to make sugar.
pyramid of numbers A diagram to show the number of living organisms present at each trophic level in an ecosystem.
radiation Energy that travels as a wave and requires no physical medium to carry it, for example light, radio waves or infra-red radiation.
refraction A change in the direction of a lightbeam caused when the light crosses from one medium to another, for example when passing from air into a glass prism the lightbeam seems to bend.
resistance The amount that a conductor prevents the flow of electric current.
respiration The chemical process that makes energy from food in the cells in your body. All living things must respire.
saturate A saturated solution is one that cannot dissolve any more solute.
sedimentary rock Rock formed when sediments from other rocks are laid down and compacted together.
solid An object with a fixed shape and volume, for example a lump of steel. Solids cannot be compressed easily into a smaller space.
solubility How easily something will dissolve.
solute Something that dissolves in a liquid to form a solution.
solvent The liquid that dissolves a solute to make a solution.
species A group of living things. Humans belong to the species *Homo sapiens*.
suspension Particles held in suspension do not sink in a liquid.
tissue A group of cells of the same type, so nervous tissue contains only nerve cells.
transluscent Allows light to pass through but the image is degraded so that you cannot clearly see through it.
transparent Allows light to pass through and form a clear image.
upthrust The force that pushes up on an object floating in water. If the weight of the object is greater than the upthrust the object will sink.
vaccination Vaccinations are specially-weakened microorganisms that your body can practise against. When the real one tries to get in you can destroy it before it makes you ill.
vacuole A sac in a cell filled with a watery solution. Plant cells tend to have large vacuoles but animal cells have small ones.
variation The existence of a range of individuals of the same group with different characteristics.
vein A blood vessel carrying blood towards the heart.
vertebrate An animal with a boney backbone or spine.
virus A tiny living organism that can cause some diseases.
weathering Rock is weathered when wind, rain, temperature changes, or living organisms break it into smaller pieces.
weight The force of gravity acting on a body on the Earth. Since weight is a force, it is measured in Newtons. People often use the word weight to mean mass but this is not strictly correct.

ANSWERS TO ACTIVITIES FOR WEEKS 1-8

Week 1 Monday

1 Three answers from: nerve cells, blood cells, skin cells, sex cells.
2 They only contain half the information needed to make copies. They cannot copy themselves.
3 They are all of the same type.
4 True
5 They all have a nucleus, cytoplasm and at least one vacuole.
6 Plant cells have a strong wall rather than a membrane. They have a large vacuole instead of several very small vacuoles.
7 Animal cell: **A** - nucleus **B** - vacuole **C** - membrane **D** - cytoplasm
Plant cell: **A** - nucleus **B** - vacuole **C** - cell wall **D** - cytoplasm
8 They contain many cells (unicellular organisms only have one cell).
9 sperm; ovule; ovum; pollen grain.
10 It gives the plant rigidity. (Animals have a skeleton.)

Week 1 Tuesday

1 Breasts enlarge; increase in body hair; shape changes; ovulation and menstruation begins; there are emotional and behavioural changes.
2 Penis increases in size; increase in body hair; voice deepens; testes produce sperm; there are emotional and behavioural changes.
3 The sperm needs the enzymes to break through the wall of the ovum (unfertilised egg) to fertilise it.
4 The sperm may not penetrate through the wall of an ovum, or there may be no ovum to fertilise because the woman is at a particular part of her cycle.
5 The placenta acts as the interface between the mother and the fetus, providing nutrition to the baby and removing waste.
6 ovulation - the process of releasing an immature egg
menstruation - monthly bleeding when the uterus lining is shed
ovary - the place where immature eggs are stored
uterus - the place where a fertilised egg embeds itself to grow
ovum - an unfertilised egg
ova - a number of unfertilised eggs
7 **A** - ovary **B** - oviduct **C** - uterus **D** - vagina
8 **A** – bladder **B** - penis **C** - testis **D** - scrotum

Week 1 Wednesday

1 Desert - hot and dry (though some are cold and dry); Rainforest - hot and wet; Northern hills - cold and wet; Arctic tundra - cold and dry.
2(a) It has thick fur to provide insulation; it is white to provide camouflage.
(b) It has broad feet so it does not sink into sand; it can store fat and water in its humps; it has a thick coat to protect it against the Sun's heat. **(c)** It breathes through gills, so it never has to surface to breathe; its fins and shape allow it to move through water quickly.
3(a) It has a long narrow beak so it can reach the nectar in a flower; it can also hover by the flower. **(b)** It is fast, has claws, sharp teeth and is camouflaged; it has eyes at the front which allow it to gauge distances well. **(c)** It is fast moving; it has eyes on either side of its head so it can see a large area.
4(a) Producer - grass Consumer - gazelle Prey - gazelle
Predator - cheetah Carnivore - cheetah Herbivore - gazelle
(b) a food chain
5(a)

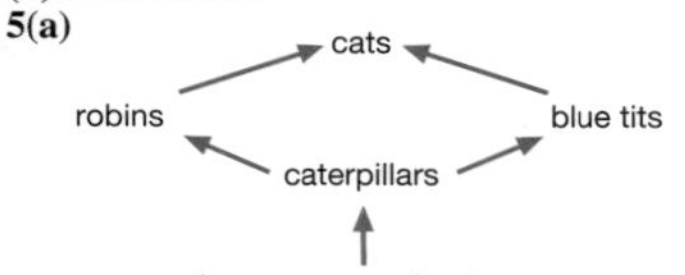

Week 1 Thursday

1 Mammal - blue whale, human, flying squirrel; Reptile - snake, crocodile; Bird - parrot; Fish - plaice; Insect - cockroach.
2 Backbone - human, dog, cat, whale; No backbone - snail, slug, ant, jellyfish.
3 The natural colour of your hair - genes; How tall you are - genes and environment; Your blood group - genes; How fast you can run - genes and environment.
4(a)

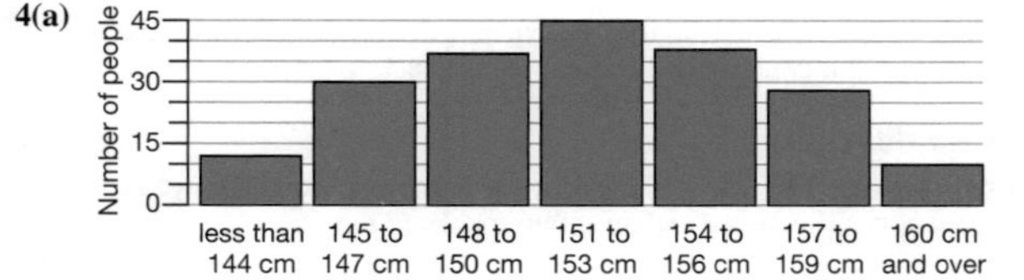

(b) Total who are 154 cm tall or taller = 76 out of 200 = 38%
38% of 20 000 000 = 7 600 000 people, so the number of women in the group will be approximately 3 800 000
5(a) The data could be repesented in a pie chart or a bar chart. **(b)** The number is approximately 56 000 000 x 2/23 = 4 869 565

Week 1 Friday

1 Three answers from: vinegar, sulphuric acid, citric acid, hydrochloric acid.
2 Three answers from: sodium hydroxide, bleach, paint stripper, cleaners.
3 pH 13 - strong alkali; pH 7.3 - weak alkali; pH 2 - strong acid; pH 7 - neutral; pH 6.6 - weak acid
4(a) A solution of bleach with a pH of 8 - 1 hydrogen ion to 100 000 000 water molecules
(b) A solution of sulphuric acide with a pH of 4 - 1 hydrogen ion to 10 000 water molecules
5 **A** - pH 2 **B** - pH 7 **C** - pH 14
6(a) Tick Use lots of water to dilute it as much as possible. **(b)** If you use an alkali, you will not know what proportion to use it in. Mopping it up will leave some residue.

Week 2 Monday

1 One answer from: change in temperature, colour, weight or characteristics of the reactants.
2 Gas may be released and it gets hotter/colder.
3(a) calcium carbonate and hydrochloric acid **(b)** calcium chloride, water and carbon dioxide
(c) magnesium carbonate + hydrochloric acid → magnesium chloride + water + carbon dioxide
(d) The carbon dioxide has been released and lost from the reactants.
4(a) hydrogen + nitrogen → ammonia **(b)** ammonia → hydrogen + nitrogen
5(a) sodium + water → sodium hydroxide + hydrogen **(b)(i)** It fizzes / bubbles are released in the water. **(ii)** It is possible to light the gas using a lighted spill.

Week 2 Tuesday

1 The particles are close together.
2 The particles in a liquid can change position. Particles in a solid cannot change position.
3 Particles can change position.
4 The particles in a gas are far apart; in a liquid they are close together.
5(a) melting **(b)** evaporation **(c)** freezing **(d)** condensing
6 The particles in a gas are far apart, but in a liquid they are close together, so they cannot be brought closer.
7(a) The gas particles slow because they are cooler. They do not hit the sides of the balloon as hard, so the pressure reduces and the balloon gets smaller.
(b) The gas particles will gain heat energy, move faster and the pressure will rise, possibly making the aerosol explode. **(c)** As they gain heat energy, the particles move more rapidly and the bonds between the particles are stretched. This makes the substances increase in size.
8(a) The mercury will move further along the tube for the same temperature change making it easier to see the change. **(b)** The narrow tube is difficult to see and the range of the thermometer is small – but if it were larger, it would be too large to hold.

Week 2 Wednesday

1(a) water **(b)** sugar
2(a) white spirit **(b)** paint
3 insoluble
4 In solutions, the particles are very small whereas in suspensions the particles are much larger – large enough to stop light passing easily through the liquid, so it appears cloudy.
5 Milk on its own is a mixture of substances. However, providing there are no other substances in the milk, it is pure (like pure sugar or pure honey).
6 **A** - chromatography; **B** - distillation; **C** - distillation; **D** - chromatography; **E** - evaporation
7(a) Tick **B** Air dissolved in the water is coming out of solution. **(b)** Air is dissolved in the water. As the water turns to ice, air comes out of solution but cannot escape, so it is trapped as bubbles.
8 The hot water and salt mixture was a **saturated solution**. The water was the **solvent** and the salt was the **solute**. The **solubility** of the water reduces as the temperature falls, so the salt comes out of **solution** and settles on the bottom of the beaker.

Week 2 Thursday

1 oil; gas; coal.
2 Three answers from: wind; tides; solar; hydroelectricity; biomass.
3 carbon dioxide
4 the Sun
5 When they burn, they release pollution such as carbon dioxide. This damages the Earth's climate.
6 They take up a lot of space and can be unsightly.
7(a) They do not pollute the city as much. If there is a problem it will affect fewer people. **(b)** It is not easy for workers to reach them. The energy they generate must be transported to the towns, which is expensive.
8 Three answers from: insulate windows, lofts and doors; walk instead of using a car; reduce the temperature of the central heating in your house.

Week 2 Friday

1 Variable resistor; buzzer; light bulb.
2 **A** - There is a wire 'shorting out' the bulb and power supply **B** - One of the batteries is pointing the wrong way **C** - There is a break in the circuit.
3(a)

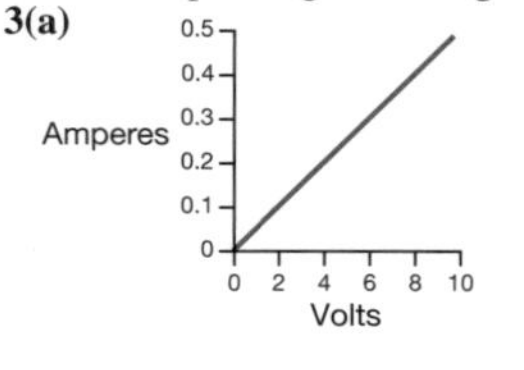

(b) 0.6 A **(c)** 3.0 V **(d)** Answer **(c)** would be unchanged; however, as the current increases, a bulb gets hotter and its resistance changes, so the answer to **(b)** might change.

Week 3 Monday

1 Tick the first diagram only which shows balanced forces.
2 850 N
3 900 N
4 If they can reduce the friction, their boat will travel faster for the same amount of force.
5 Average speed is 32 / 4 = 8 kmph
6 Average speed is 150 / 6 = 25 mps
7 In space there is no air, so there is no air resistance; therefore, the satellite can be any shape. Planes are streamlined, so less energy is needed to travel at the same speed.
8

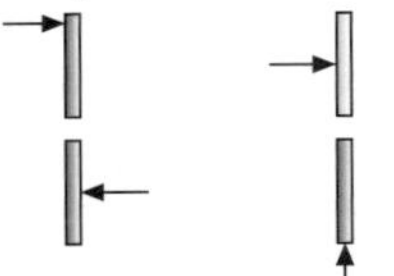

Week 3 Tuesday

1(a) 4 x 1 cm = 4 cm **(b)** 110 x 4 cm = 440 cm
2 The shadow of the Earth is larger than the shadow of the Moon, so it is rare that the shadow of the Moon passes over us and we see an eclipse of the Sun. If the Moon passes into the shadow of the Earth, half of the world can view the eclipse.
3 the Moon
4 the Sun
5 star; planet; satellite.
6 Tick False. (It is because the Sun is a long way from us.)
7 1 winter 2 orbit 3 Sun 4 tilt 5 Earth
8

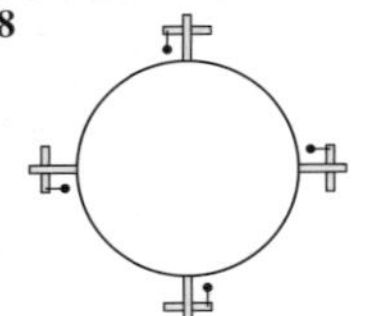

Week 3 Wednesday

1 Our bodies need a wide range of nutrients to grow healthily. These can only be obtained from eating a balanced diet.
2 They still need to repair cells and replace cells, even though they are not adding to their bodies. They also need energy.
3 It helps to keep the muscles in your gut strong, so you do not suffer from bowel problems in later life.
4 Smaller lumps react faster with a liquid than large lumps because there is more surface area. Chewing your food therefore makes your digestion more efficient. During chewing, you add digestive substances to the food, so it is already being broken down before it reaches your stomach.
5 The intestine is not absorbing water from your food.
6 The digestive substances in your body are acidic. When they come into contact with your teeth they react with them and cause decay.
7 They will not be able to reabsorb the water they added to food during the digestive process. They are likely to need to drink more water.

Week 3 Thursday

1 A - trachea; **B** - bronchus; **C** - lungs.
2 glucose + **oxygen** → **carbon dioxide** + water
3 oxygen
4 carbon dioxide
5 False – only a small proportion leaves your body each time.
6 False – arteries carry blood away from your heart. It returns in the veins.
7 True
8(a) in your red blood cells **(b)** to carry oxygen
9 Both effects help to transport more oxygen around your body and remove carbon dioxide faster.
10 All your cells need oxygen to live. If the haemoglobin is not carrying as much oxygen, you must breathe harder to carry the same amount to your cells.

Week 3 Friday

1 Microbes help us to make bread, yoghurt and other foods.
2 Microbes cause infectious diseases.
3 an epidemic
4 Contagious diseases are passed on by direct contact between people. Infectious diseases spread through air or water.
5 A virus enters a cell and makes the cell reproduce copies of it.
6 Antibodies recognise viruses and destroy them. If you have been vaccinated for a particular disease, you already have the antibodies to fight a virus if it tries to infect you.
7 Bacteria reproduce faster at higher temperatures, so keeping the food cool means the bacteria do not reproduce quickly and make the food go 'off'.
8 Two answers from: be hygienic – wash your hands after you have been to the toilet; sterilise surfaces and objects; use antiseptics.
9 The inoculation introduces a small amount of the measle virus into your body. Your body produces the necessary antibodies to fight it when you are infected by the virus.
10 The number of bacteria is doubling every five minutes. You will find it easier to use a calculator because the numbers get large.
30 minutes – 64
60 minutes – 4 096
120 minutes – 16 777 216

Week 4 Monday

1(a)(i) vegetation **(ii)** worm, snail **(iii)** hedgehog, vole, owl, fox **(iv)** hedgehog, vole, owl, fox
(b) The number of hedgehogs and voles may rise. This might result in more owls and fewer worms and snails. **(c)** There might be more worms as they could find more food. Voles and hedgehogs would need to eat only worms instead of snails, so the number of worms would then reduce.
2 They move to where food is more plentiful, and where they do not need to use as much energy keeping warm.
3 Reducing their body temperature and activity level saves energy at a time when food is scarce.
4(a) There is less sunlight in winter, so there is less foliage and fewer plants.
(b) There is less for primary consumers to eat, so they may migrate or die.
(c) They have larger bodies, so can have a larger store of energy than primary consumers. They can cope with eating less. They may also hibernate to save energy.
5 Transects or quadrats may be used to estimate proportions of different plants.

Week 4 Tuesday

1 Elements: hydrogen and oxygen. All others are not elements
2

	oxygen	hydrogen	helium	gold
gas at room temperature	yes	yes	yes	no
solid at room temperature	no	no	no	yes
metal	no	no	no	yes
explosive	no	yes	no	no

3

	wood	expanded polystyrene	paper	glass
flammable	yes	yes	yes	no
less dense than water	yes	yes	yes	no
transparent	no	no	no	yes

4 For atoms to link together to become compounds they must come close together and form bonds.
5 C – carbon; H – hydrogen; He – helium; O – oxygen; Cl – chlorine; N – nitrogen; Pb – lead
6 There are two hydrogen atoms bonded to a single oxygen atom in a single water molecule.

Week 4 Wednesday

1(a) C **(b)** O **(c)** H
2(a) NaCl **(b)** H_2O **(c)** CO_2
3 An element contains only one kind of atom, whereas a compound contains more than one type.
4 In a compound the atoms are bonded together. They need a chemical reaction to separate them. In a mixture the substances may be together, but they are not bonded.
5(a) Sand is a mixture. **(b)** You do not need a chemical reaction to separate the salt and grit.
6(a) Concrete is a mixture. **(b)** The concrete can be crushed and sieved to separate the sand from the gravel. You do not need a chemical reaction.
7(a) carbon (charcoal) + oxygen → carbon dioxide
(b) Elements: carbon and oxygen; compound: carbon dioxide.
(c) carbon – C; oxygen – O; carbon dioxide = CO_2.

Week 4 Thursday

1 C B A
2 B C A
3 One answer from: the water and rock cause a chemical reaction; a rough sea throws rocks at the cliff face knocking bits off.
4 transportation
5 sedimentation
6 Heating the rock causes the rock to expand. Cooling a section of the rock causes that part to contract and this causes the rock to break.

Week 4 Friday

1(a) sedimentary **(b)** The small creatures would have been destroyed by heat and temperature if it was a metamorphic rock.
2 metamorphic
3(a) roofs **(b)** It was formed as layers, so it can be split along those layers forming large flat sheets of rock.
4(a) One answer from: statues; buildings; work surfaces. **(b)** One answer from: buildings; road building; making cement.
5 Lava is molten rock that has reached the Earth's surface. Magma is molten rock that is still beneath the ground.
6 A = magma; **B** = Metamorphic; **C** = igneous; **D** = lava; **E** = Magma; **F** = Igneous; **G** = sedimentary; **H** = Sedimentary; **I** = metamorphic; **J** = sedimentary; **K** = metamorphic; **L** = sedimentary.

Week 5 Monday

1 Shiny surfaces are poor emitters of heat radiation, so less heat is wasted if the kettle has a shiny surface.
2(a) conduction **(b)** The material contains pockets of air, and air is a poor conductor of heat.

3 Polystyrene is a poor conductor of heat. The lid stops heat from being lost by convection.
4(a) The heat sink has a large surface area so it can radiate heat energy easily. The fins are angled so they radiate into the air, not to another fin.
(b) Matt black surfaces emit heat radiation efficiently.
5 The large heat sink conducts heat away from the microprocessor. The large surface area means the heat can be radiated efficiently. The moving air takes heat energy away from the heat sink.
6 The tray will be larger when it is warm than when it is cold, so it will push against the sides of the cooker.
7 Air is a poor conductor of heat. Trapping air in a fabric makes the fabric a good heat insulator.

Week 5 Tuesday

1 False (steel can be used to make a permanent magnet).
2 solenoid
3 core
4 Heat it. / Hit (vibrate) it so the atoms are rearranged.
5 Increase the number of coils. / Increase the size of the electric current.
6

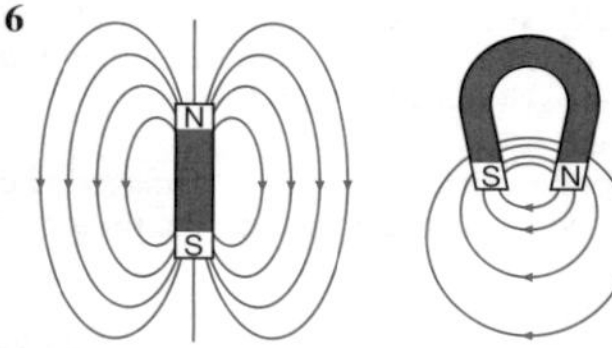

7 True
8 When the button is pressed, current flows through the coil of the electromagnet. The electromagnet becomes magnetic. It pulls the steel arm to the left. The hammer strikes the bell to make a sound. As it does so, the electric contacts break – so the electromagnet switches off. The steel springs back to the right. The contact is made again and the situation repeats.

Week 5 Wednesday

1 A translucent material allows light through, but you cannot see objects clearly through it.
2 A transparent material allows light through **and** you can see objects clearly through it.
3 Tick It must be opaque.
4(a) B (b) A
5 Tick It absorbs some light. Tick It reflects some light.
6 Tick It is opaque.
7

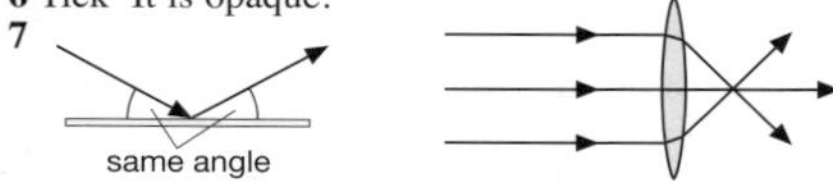

Week 5 Thursday

1(a) A (b) B (c) B (d) B (e) C
2

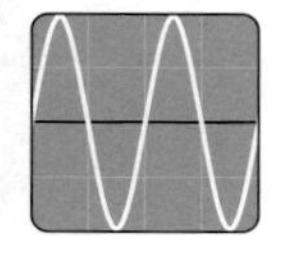

3(a) noise pollution **(b)** Build a barrier by the side of the road, such as a high fence, trees or a high earth bank.
4 outer ear / ear drum / inner ear / cochlea

Week 5 Friday

1 inherited characteristics
2(a) The baby will inherit some genes from each parent that will make her a good runner. **(b)** Their baby may have an accident / may get a disease / may not train properly / may not eat well.
3 You need to be able to select the animal or plant with the characteristics you want. If the animals/plants are all the same, there is no reason to choose one instead of another.
4

natural hair colour	genes	
skin colour	genes	
weight	genes	environment
footballing skills	genes	environment
actual hair colour	genes	environment
eye colour	genes	
height	genes	environment
hair length	genes	environment

5 **A** = 5 **B** = 4 **C** = 6 **D** = 3 **E** = 1 **F** = 2

Week 6 Monday

1 circulatory system / respiratory system
2 respiratory system
3 digestive system
4 protection / mobility
5 takes in oxygen / removes carbon dioxide
6 False – veins carry the blood back.
7 nicotine
8 Carbon dioxide (which is a poison) will build up in their body. Also, there will be no oxygen for respiration.
9 There is no blood flow carrying nutrients and oxygen to the brain.
10 carbon dioxide / blood vessel / oxygen

Week 6 Tuesday

1 carbon dioxide + water → **oxygen** + starch
2 oxygen and carbon dioxide
3 Tick the water. Tick the air (carbon)
4 Animals breathe oxygen and they must get rid of carbon dioxide. The starch is the source of energy for them.
5(a) Light is needed for the plants to photosynthesise. **(b)** The carbon dioxide level in the water would increase and there would be less to eat. Both would affect the health of the fish. (Note: In this tank, the air pump will ensure there is oxygen in the water.)

Week 6 Wednesday

1 e.g. wheat; rice; potatoes; carrots; peas; cauliflower; lettuce, etc.
2 e.g. cows; sheep; pigs; chickens; rabbits; turkeys, etc.
3 e.g. tuna; shark; cod.
4 At each level of a food chain, energy is 'lost' as the animals use the energy to move, stay warm and to breed. The fewer layers there are, the greater the proportion of energy that reaches the top layer (humans).
5 In some areas, the soil is so poor that crops will not grow. People must eat animals that graze on the vegetation and keep moving so the animals have enough to eat.
6(a) Removing hedges increases the size of fields and makes them easier to farm with large machinery. **(b)** There is a reduction in biodiversity as there are fewer places for animals to live and to breed. There can be greater soil erosion. **(c)** The price of foods may rise.
7(a) There will be fewer insects, so fewer small birds. As a result there will be fewer large birds. **(b)** There will be fewer nesting places for the small birds, and less cover for the small animals. The number of insects might increase. There are likely to be fewer large birds. **(c)** Fewer hawks would lead to more small birds, mice and rabbits. As a result they would eat more crops.

Week 6 Thursday

1 good conductors of heat and electricity; shiny; can be shaped by hitting them.
2 e.g. iron Fe; copper Cu; lead Pb.
3 Rust is iron oxide.
4 Marble and limestone are calcium carbonate.
5 metal salt (and water)
6 carbon dioxide
7(a) metal + water → **metal hydroxide + hydrogen (b)** metal oxide + water → **metal hydroxide (c)** metal + acid → **metal salt + hydrogen**
(d) metal oxide + acid → **metal salt + water (e)** metal carbonate + acid → **metal salt + water + carbon dioxide**
8 calcium carbonate + hydrochloric acid → calcium chloride + water + carbon dioxide
9 sodium oxide + water → sodium hydroxide
10 copper oxide + sulphuric acid → copper sulphate + water

Week 6 Friday

1(a) Aluminium is more reactive than iron, so it competes for the oxygen with the iron – and wins. **(b)** competition reaction
2 Gold is less reactive, so it stays bright. Copper would react with the air.
3(a) It always made a good electrical contact because it did not build up a layer of oxide. **(b)** Copper is much cheaper than gold.
4 Copper nails do not react with sea water as quickly as iron nails do, so copper nails last longer.
5 potassium calcium copper platinum
6 sodium aluminium zinc copper gold
7(a) gold – found as an element in rock; aluminium – using electricity; iron – heating it with carbon.
(b) Silver is often found as an element.
8 Sodium and potassium would react with moisture in the air if they came in contact with it. Therefore, they are stored under oil.

Week 7 Monday

1 pollution from factories; pollution from power plants; pollution from vehicles
2 water that is on or in the ground (in soil or rocks), as opposed to rainwater
3 Add crushed limestone to the lake.
4 Snow and ice melt releasing large amounts of acidic water, which fell and was frozen in the winter.
5 Acid rain can cause fish to die. Birds that live on the fish will also die.
6 Some rocks react more with acid rain than others. Buildings made from limestone will be affected more than those made from granite.
7 The underlying rocks determine the acidity of the soil. Some plants grow best in certain types of soil, so by seeing which plants are growing best we can determine the kind of rock.

Week 7 Tuesday

1(a) exothermic reaction **(b)** Because it is a reaction that releases heat energy.
2(a) Heat energy has been released and the substance's properties have changed. **(b)** exothermic reaction
3 three (magnesium, sulphur and oxygen)
4(a) four (sodium, hydrogen, carbon, oxygen) **(b)** steam **(c)** It can taste soapy.
5(a) Heat has been released, and the substance's properties have changed.
(b) The magnesium has reacted with oxygen, so there are now more atoms in the substance.

Week 7 Wednesday

1(a) chemical energy **(b)** electrical energy
2 **A** – 2 **B** – 3 **C** – 5 **D** – 1 **E** – 4

3 Energy can be transferred from one form to another, but can never be created or destroyed.
4 They produce pollution; there is a limited supply.
5(a) True and false **(b)** True, because it does not produce pollution when it is used. False, because it still has to be generated – and this causes pollution.
6 It is popular because it is very versatile; it can be used to produce motion, sound, heat, etc.
7(a) C (b) B (c) A

Week 7 Thursday

1 A - 3 **B** - 4 **C** - 1 **D** - 2
2 no satellite television; no satellite navigation; problems with phone calls; poor weather reports, etc.
3(a) C (b) A (c) B
4 The distances are so large – astronauts would be old by the time they reached the planets. It is also safer and cheaper not to use astronauts.
5 Tick **A** By 2003 it had passed the Moon. Tick **B** By 2003 it had passed through the asteroid belt. Tick **C** By 2003 it had passed the outer planets.

Week 7 Friday

1 Crouching reduces air resistance so they can travel faster for the same effort.
2 A snowflake does not weigh as much as a raindrop. This means that the air resistance can match the weight of the snowflake at a slower speed. Snowflakes are flat so they are not as streamlined as raindrops.
3 Above the water: when the oar is horizontal, there is little drag on the oar, so the rower can swing it without slowing the boat. Below the water: when the oar is vertical, it has maximum drag, so it pushes more water when it moves, making the boat travel faster.
4(a) F (b) D (c) A (d) A and **F (e) B** - the amount of drag was the same (it was the same as the weight of the skydiver, so the skydiver fell at a constant speed).

Week 8 Monday

1 The wide feet reduce the pressure on the mud. As a result the bird does not sink in the mud.
2 The sharper the point is, the lower the force that is needed to produce the pressure to pierce the skin.
3 The mobile balances. Although the total weight on the left is half that on the right, the weight on the right is twice as far out.
4(a) 10 N x 150 cm = 1500 Ncm **(b)** 1500 Ncm / 10 cm = 150 N
5 pressure on left side = pressure on right side
upward force / 50 cm^2 = 2 N / 2 cm^2
upward force = 50 x 2 / 2 = 50 N

Week 8 Tuesday

1 Scientific questions are: **A**, **C** and **F**.
2(a) C (b) B and **C (c) A (d)** If doubling the temperature (in °C) doubles the amount dissolved, then values are: 20°C – 20g 40°C – 40g 80°C – 80g.
(e) At higher temperatures, the water would be boiling and at lower temperatures it would be freezing. Therefore, it is not sensible to predict beyond this range.

Week 8 Wednesday

1(a) lengths and diameters of the wires **(b)** Treat plants of the same age in similar locations; use the same dose. **(c)** dose of drug, type of ailment the patient had, age of patient **(d)** temperature inside the house, temperature and weather outside the house **(e)** Use the same bulb; try to keep the brightness the same; use fresh batteries each time. **(f)** Measure the amount of carbon dioxide the same way each time; use the same kind of yeast each time; use the same concentration of sugar each time.
2(a)(i) yes **(ii)** no **(b)(i)** no **(ii)** yes
3 There may be variations in the experiment due to time or to random events. Repeating the readings helps to get a more representative value.
4 They are data that other people have provided from their experiments. It helps a scientist to know the kinds of values they might expect from their experiment and therefore what apparatus to choose.

Week 8 Thursday

1(a) The value at 20 minutes, because it is much higher than the line of best fit.
(b) approximately 84 °C **(c)** approximately 47 °C **(d)** The temperature is varying with time, so by the time you repeat the reading the temperature will have changed. Therefore you should not average it with a previous reading. However, you could run the whole experiment from the start again.
2(a) The value at 15cm, because it is far off the line of best fit.
(b) approximately 50s **(c)** approximately 113s **(d)** It is difficult to judge the start and end of a swing. By taking the reading for 10 swings, any error in this timing gets smaller per swing. **(e)** This is a very repeatable experiment and any errors are due to the experimenter's poor reactions. This can be overcome by taking several readings and averaging them.

Week 8 Friday

1(a) 1 in 12 **(b)** 2 people
2 a reading that does not fit the pattern
3 Repeat the experiment, especially taking readings around the anomalous value to see if the value is likely to be an error or is correct.
4 They may indicate that something special has happened in a particular set of circumstances which may lead to a new discovery.
5(a) Tick **B** Be sceptical. **(b)** In your experience, the Moon does not normally change colour. **(c)** On which night and at what time did you see it happen? What colour did it go? How long did it last? Did anybody else see it? (Note: in a lunar eclipse, the Moon appears red – perhaps that is what they saw.)
6(a) Tick **B** Be sceptical. **(b)** Because a healthy diet is normally a balanced diet. **(c)** Where did you get the information? (Was it a reliable source?) What was the name of the doctor? How much weight does the doctor claim you will lose?

PRACTICE TEST ANSWERS

1(a) Tick egg cell Tick sperm cell **(b)** Tick reproductive system **(c)** e.g. eye colour, natural hair colour, blood group
2(a) It ensures it is a fair test. **(b)(i)** mm **(ii)** The groups overlap; for example, somebody with feet that were 160 mm long would appear in two groups and would be counted twice. **(c)** Tick Observe pupils' ear lobes **(d)** The bar for attached ear lobes goes up to 12 pupils. **(e)** The total of 12 + 7 (19) for the ear lobe experiment is less than the total bars for the foot experiment (even allowing for the overlap).
3(a)(i) nutrients **(ii)** carbon dioxide **(b)(i)** heart **(ii)** It stops nutrients reaching organs; it prevents harmful substances from being removed; it stops the blood flowing, so the cells beyond the blockage die.
4(a) It is not a good conductor of electricity. It is not a good conductor of heat. **(b)** If some of the substance dissolves into water and leaves a residue that was not dissolved, then it is not a pure substance (it must be a mixture).
(c) filtration **(d)** The water has evaporated.
5(a)(i) Bone **A** moves as the eardrum vibrates. **(ii)** If the bone is damaged, the vibrations of the eardrum will not be passed to the inner ear – so the person will not hear. **(b)(i)** bat, cat, dog **(ii)** human
6(a) Plan **B** is more detailed. It clearly says what will happen in the experiment. **(b)** Be careful not to drop the masses on your foot. Do not let bits of broken plastic go into your eye. Wear goggles. **(c)** The others have sharp corners, so they may not fall onto each case in exactly the same way. It will not matter how you drop the spherical mass; it will hit the cases in the same way each time. **(d)(i)** results **(ii) most protective** clam folder crystal **least protective**
7(a) Aluminium is a metal, so it is a good conductor of electricity. **(b)** Paper is not a conductor of electricity. **(c)(i)** The filament in the bulb is broken. **(ii)** One of the batteries is the wrong way round. **(d)** The battery ran out of chemical energy, so it was 'flat'.
8(a) A and **C (b) A** and **C (c) B (d)** gravity – the weight of the child **(e)** air resistance **(f)** When the swing moves from **A** to **B**, most of the **gravitational potential** energy turns into **kinetic** energy. Some energy is also transferred into **thermal** energy.

Awarding a level for the practice test

Work out your total score. Use the table to work out the level you have achieved in **this test**. This is only a guide to the level at which you are working but should give you an idea of how you could expect to perform in the Tests.

Level	Marks
N	0–6
3	7–12
4	13–21
5	22–33
6	34–44